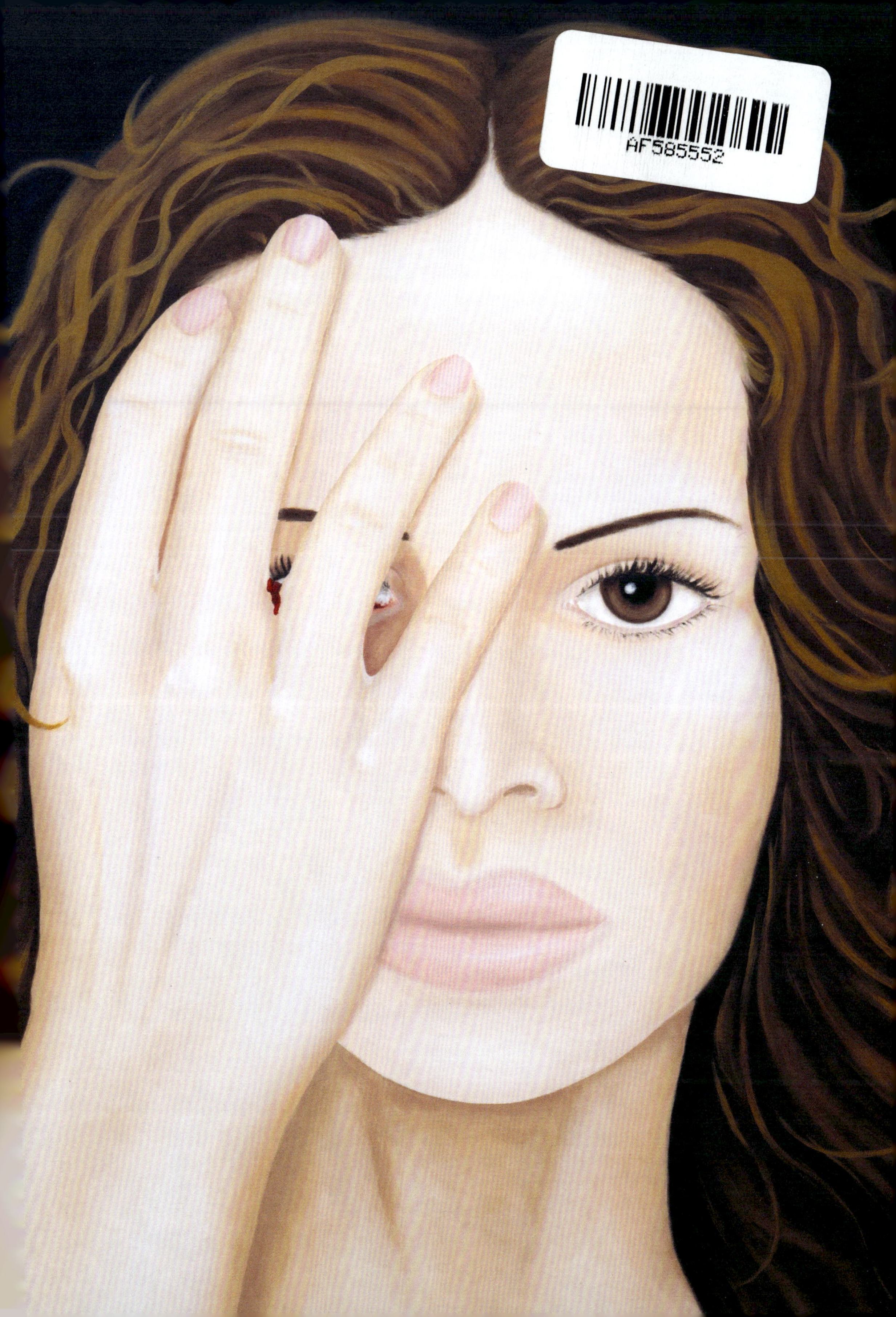

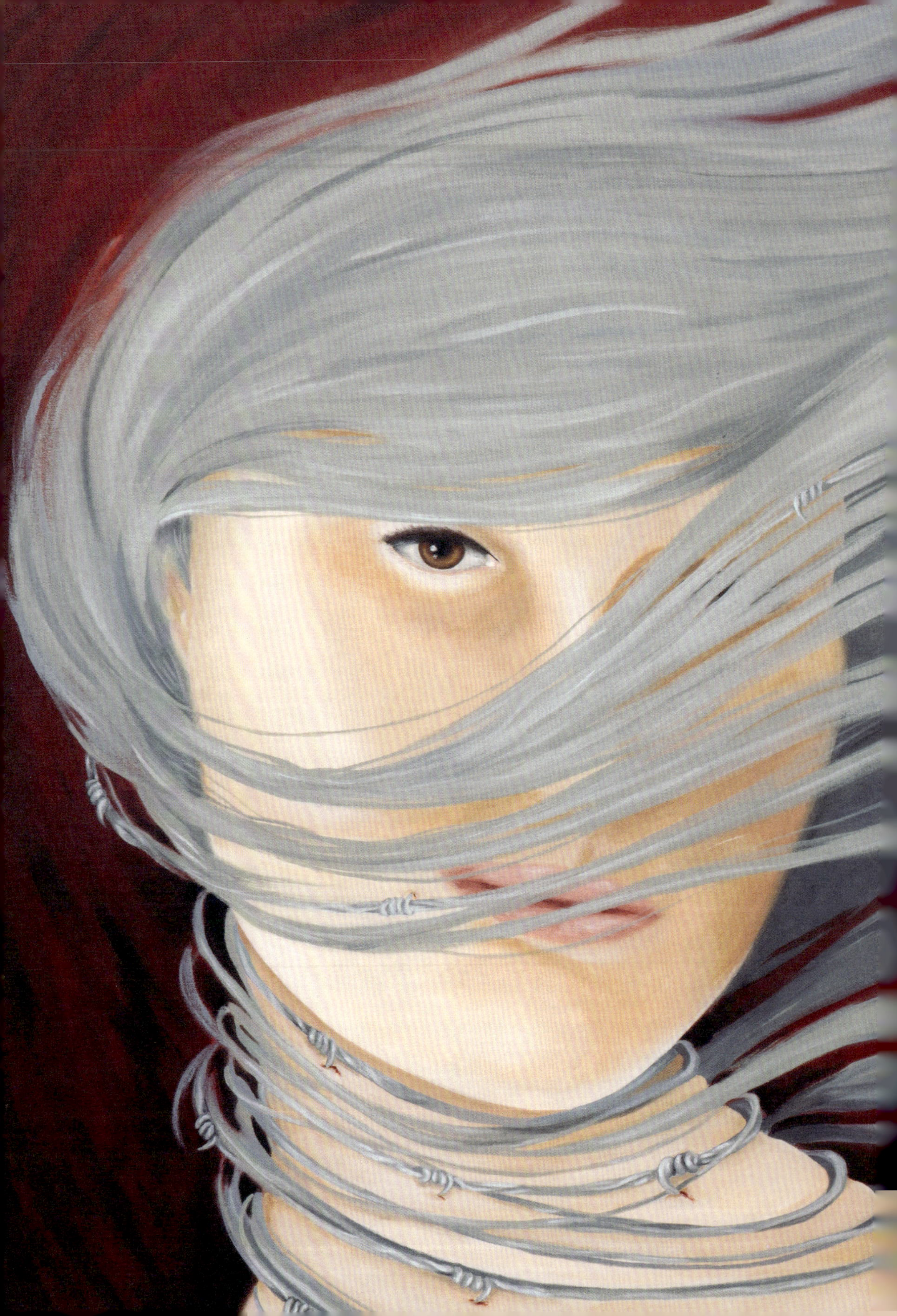

FROM THE OTHER SIDE

From the other side

Australian Centre for Contemporary Art
9 December 2023 – 3 March 2024

Naomi Blacklock
Mia Boe
Louise Bourgeois
Cybele Cox
Theron Debris
Karla Dickens
Lonnie Hutchinson
Naomi Kantjuriny
Minyoung Kim
Maria Kozic
Jemima Lucas
Clare Milledge
Tracey Moffatt
Julia Robinson
Marianna Simnett
Heather B Swann
Suzan Pitt
Kellie Wells
Zamara Zamara

Curated by Elyse Goldfinch and Jessica Clark

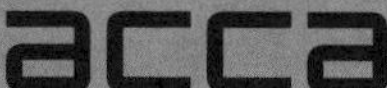

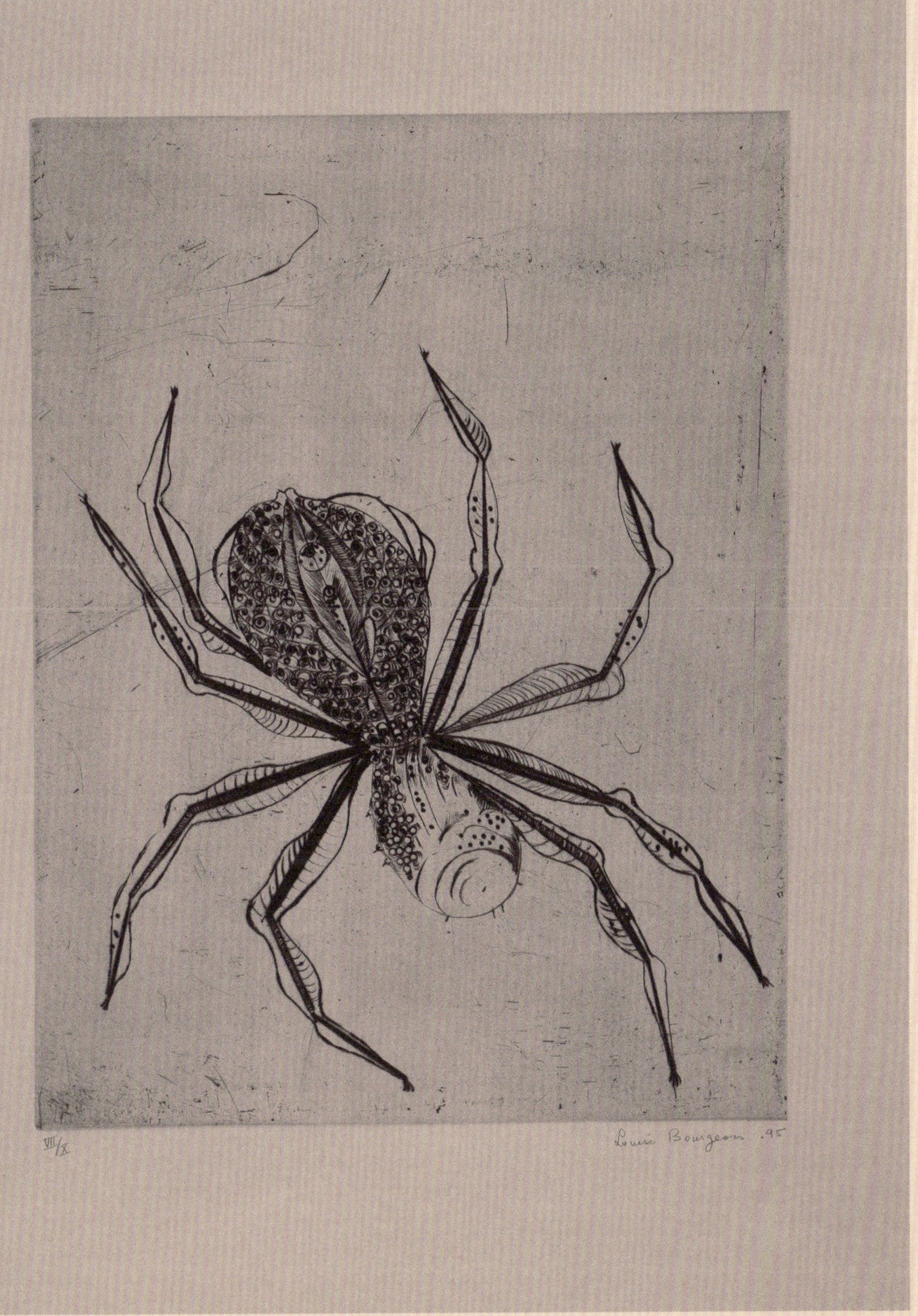

Contents

Advisory note: Horror confronts us with feelings of fear, dread, and unease as a way of helping us cope with the uncomfortable realities of the everyday. This publication similarly contains material that may be sensitive and challenging including written descriptions of and references to violence, abuse and sexual assault.

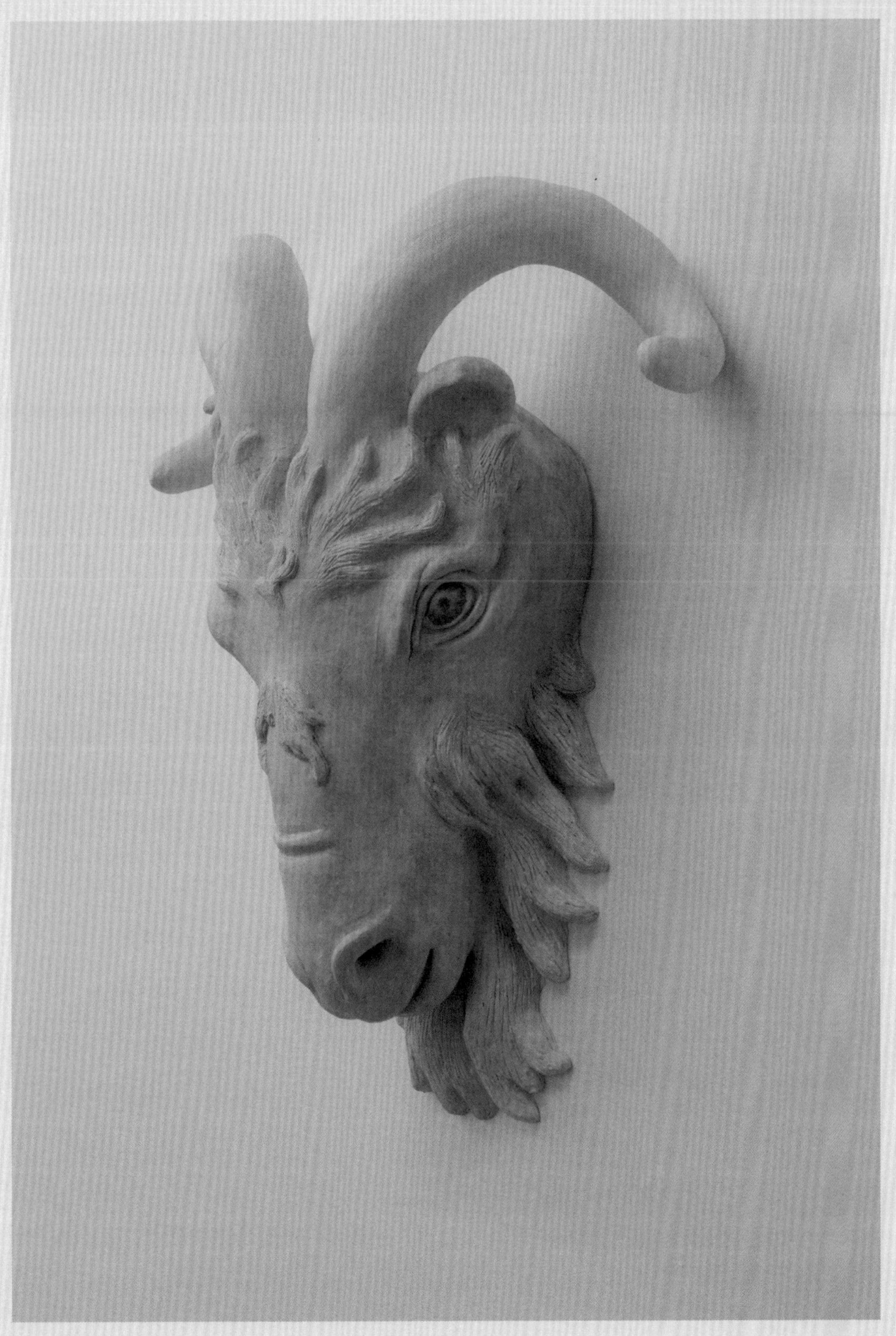

Notes from the Editor

Elyse Goldfinch

From the other side was born of a desire to investigate the productive powers of horror, particularly from the perspective of those who have historically been subjugated to the roles of monsters, or worse victims, by overwhelmingly male creators. Playing in the proverbial muck of the genre, co-curator Jessica Clark and I have gorged ourselves on every horror film, text and podcast we could get our hands on, alongside endless conversations with other spellbound and curious artists, colleagues and friends. During the exhibition's development, we quickly realised we weren't interested in trying to (re)define what horror is, rather, what horror *does*. Horror confronts and contaminates; it empowers the powerless; it gives form to our anxieties and desires; it exorcises our darkest fears; it creeps its way into the body and lingers, becoming internalised. Horror is a feeling, a release.

With the aim to transgress and dismantle social stereotypes and traditional narratives of the body, race, gender, sexuality, desire, pleasure and rage, the exhibition and publication come together to embrace horror's slipperiness, its refusal to be neatly categorised. They attempt to make us *feel* the way we do when we *feel* horror – from terror to tenderness, vulnerability and protection.

Alongside introductory essays by Jessica Clark and myself that further unpack our curatorial motivations, and speak to the works in the exhibition, contributions by leading writers in the field expand on horror's capacity as a liberating, rebellious force.

Cinema Studies Professor, Barbara Creed introduces her theory of the monstrous-feminine and investigates how the genre has evolved since the original publication in 1993. Author Lisa Fuller's short story is told from the perspective of a young woman about to come of age, but she discovers that becoming an adult means a much more 'monstrous' transformation than she could have predicted. Academic Jessica Balanzategui reflects on how the intersections between art and horror films operate as a platform for women's and marginalised voices, exploring horror as a space of healing and potentiality. Cult-figure Kier-La Janisse deploys Kate Millet's *The Basement* as a case-study to explore how female violence against 'other' women is depicted in fiction, particularly by female authors. Janisse considers the wider reception of these types of stories in cultural movements from second-wave feminism to the phenomenon of true-crime obsession. Finally, screen writer Alison Peirse explores the various shared and individual experiences of watching horror films, in a cinema with friends, or at home alone. In diary form, she unpacks how consuming horror through fiction can help us navigate the real horrors of the world around us.

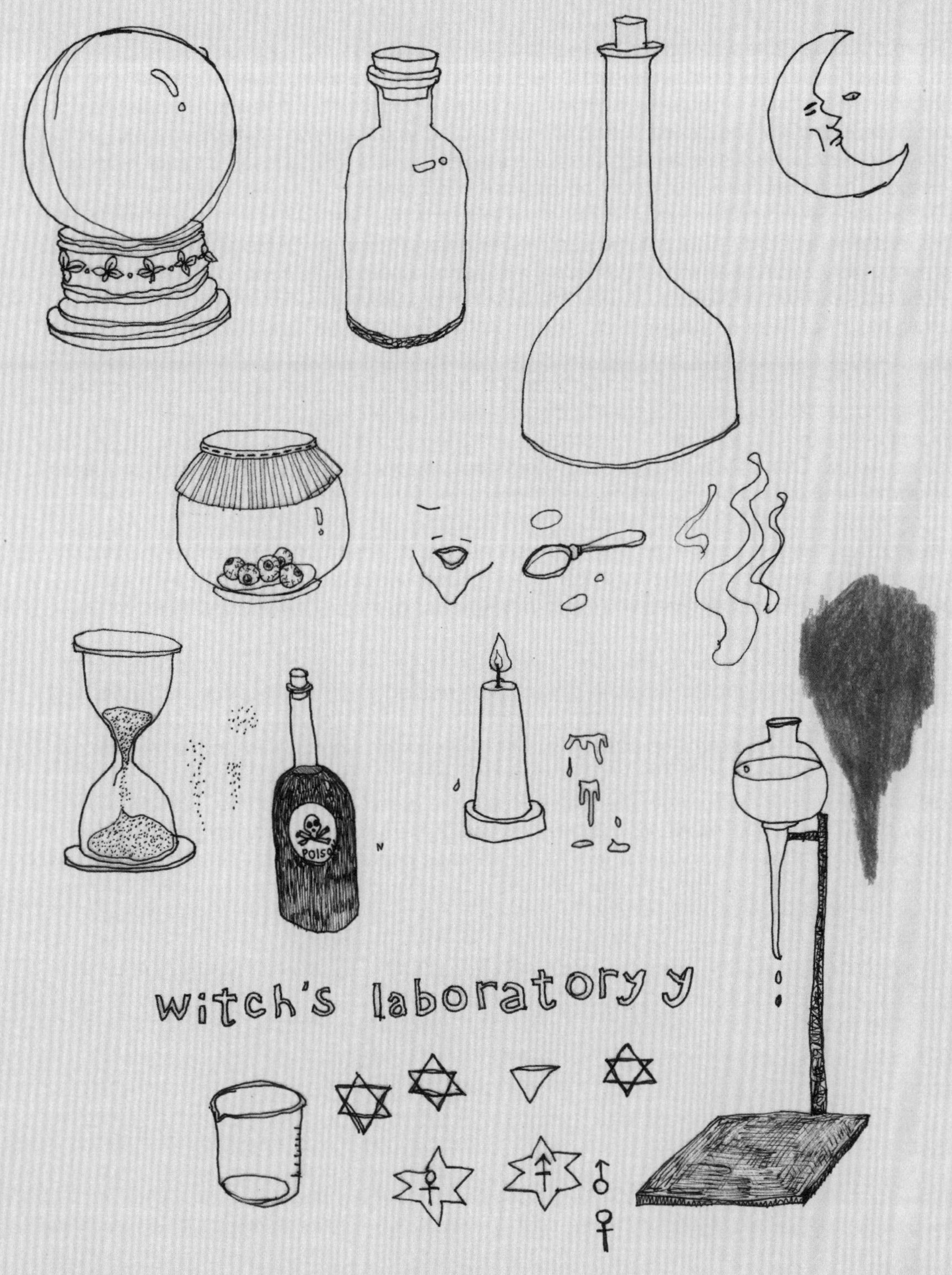
POISO
witch's laboratoryy

From the other side: Introduction

Elyse Goldfinch and Jessica Clark

Horror often speaks to the collective anxieties and fears of our times, from sexual liberation to new technologies, racial tension to gender subversion. This fear proliferates across shared cultural imaginaries to lay bare our innermost desires, tendencies for self-destruction and the conflicting impulses to confront and exorcise our darkest fantasies. Horror provides a language with which to be scared and to respond to challenges that might be beyond our control.

From the other side brings together nineteen Australian and international artists, integrating historical and contemporary works, alongside key new commissions subjugation. The exhibition summons the impulse for rage and revenge, while embracing feelings of vulnerability and unease. Rather than speculating on the field of horror as a whole, the exhibition embeds and casts a lens upon feminist, queer and non-binary subjectivities to consider the transgressive pleasures and liberations of horror, as makers, masters and consumers of the genre.

Centring the fear of the monstrous-feminine, the exhibition raises questions about the often-harmful representation of female monsters — the witch, the hag, the monstrous mother, the shapeshifter, the possessed woman — and how she has been reclaimed by female storytellers in recent years. The monstrous-feminine resists the prototypical role of women in horror, as either victims or final girls; instead she performs the dual roles of temptress and castrator — alluring yet repulsive, contaminating yet pure.

The exhibition crosses the artificial parameters of horror in the everyday, as something that exists as part of society but also from outside of it. Culminating in a potent synthesis of dread, camp, humour and catharsis, *From the other side* challenges the traditional narratives and assumed boundaries of the body, gender, the self and the 'other'.

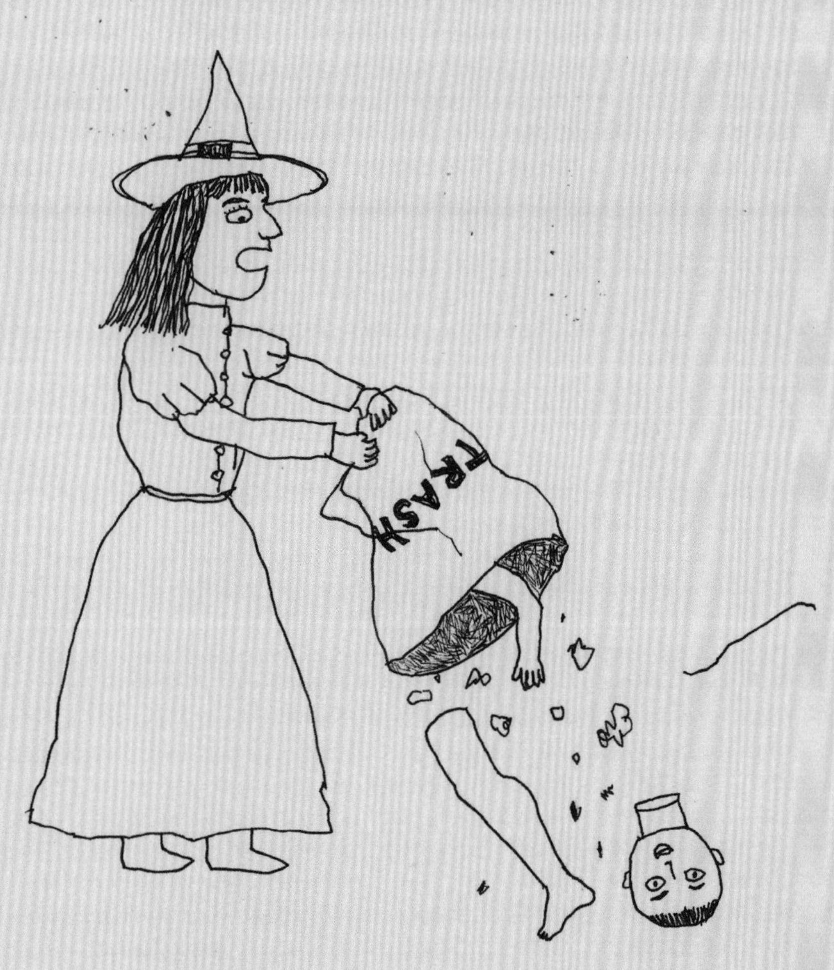
TRASH

The Monstrous-Feminine: Rage, Pleasure, Revolt
Barbara Creed

All human societies – past and present – have a concept of the monstrous-feminine, of what it is about woman that truly shocks and horrifies. Ancient myths and legends about female monsters – from Circe, Medusa, Medea, and the Sirens to the modern witch, vampire and femme fatale – focus on her terrifying powers and magical potencies. Since I first proposed the concept of the monstrous-feminine in a 1986 *Screen* article,[1] the idea has been taken up in a range of academic disciplines from cinema studies to gender studies, classics, literature, and art history. Film directors, artists, playwrights, authors and podcasters have devoted creative works to exploring her image, appeal and influence. There has also been global interest with translations and publication of books and articles on the monstrous-feminine and her uncanny pursuits in films from a range of countries.[2] This international exhibition *From the other side* is a testament to the continuing fascination she exerts. Who is the monstrous-feminine and how does she differ from male monsters? Why such interest in a misogynistic stereotype designed to warn men about woman's treacherous nature and terrifying powers – a warning intended to render women powerless in the patriarchal world? How does she, in later decades, embark on a revolt of her own?

The monstrous-feminine is particularly dominant in the horror genre of the sixties and seventies. Her rising popularity during the period of second-wave feminism in films such as *Carrie*, Brian De Palma, 1976; *The Exorcist*, William Friedkin, 1973; *Alien*, Ridley Scott, 1979; *The Brood*, David Cronenberg 1979; and *I Spit on Your Grave*, Meir Zarchi, 1978, suggests a strong association between the new more radical gender politics of the period and female-centred horror. Possibly, these films sounded a contradictory warning about feminist politics becoming too radical. Audiences nonetheless loved to watch her dismantle patriarchal society, in films such as *The Exorcist*, with its emphasis on male power and family values yet, in the end, she has to be stopped. A close analysis of these monstrous figures reveals a common theme. They are represented as monstrous because their desires, sexuality and reproductive powers are abject, and as such they threaten the patriarchal symbolic order. They menstruate, conceive, give birth, lactate, incorporate and castrate. Arguably the prototype of what constitutes the monstrous is the female sexual and reproductive body – as explored by David Cronenberg in *The Brood*, and more recently by Julia Ducournau in *Titane*, 2021. Although these monstrous women commit terrible acts of vengeance against their tormentors, audiences – particularly female spectators – find them empowering. *Carrie* is now a cult figure, despite her inevitable death, and descent into hell, because she develops terrifying telekinetic powers, brought on by her first menstruation, and is daring enough to use these to destroy her classmates who have bullied her remorselessly. Scenes of Carrie's blood mixed with pig's blood in the final apocalyptic scenes, become a source of inspiration for many female viewers. Jennifer from *I Spit on Your Grave,* who has been brutally raped by a gang of young men, kills them all – literally castrating their brutal leader in a bath, locking the door and listening to his cries for help, against a background of the aria 'Sola, perduta, abbandonata' from Puccini's *Manon Lescaut*. She is one of the few female protagonists who is not punished for her brutal revenge – although her rape constituted a savage punishment for simply being a woman. Despite her new-found affinity with acts of violence, viewers have cheered along as she exacts revenge. The film, however, has been criticised for its overly long depiction of the brutal rape scene which is seen by some as misogynistic and voyeuristic.

I Spit on Your Grave, which belongs to the rape–revenge sub-genre of horror, directly raises the question of female rage and female violence. As with her ancient counterparts, from the Sirens to Medea, the monstrous-feminine does not shy away from violence. Classic horror films and recent films about the horror of the everyday that depict female violence, such as *Trouble Everyday*, Claire Denis, 2001; *Jennifer's Body*, Karyn Kusama, 2009; *Pearl*, Ti West, 2022; *Revenge*, Coralie Fargeat, 2017; *The Nightingale*, Jennifer Kent, 2018; and *Titane*, Julia Ducournau, 2021, have frequently received incredulous responses – even dismissed as 'unfeminist'– by those who believe women are incapable of experiencing rage and committing violent acts. The monstrous-feminine challenges gender stereotypes concerning violence which is a major reason why so many female spectators find her actions so exhilarating.

I wrote *The Monstrous-Feminine: Film, Feminism, Psychoanalysis*, 1993 in order to explore more fully how patriarchal ideology has defined and shaped female monstrosity throughout the centuries from ancient myths and religion to art, film and popular culture.[3] Julia Kristeva's *Powers of Horror,* 1982 in which she presented her theory of the abject was particularly illuminating in understanding why patriarchal societies have over the centuries constructed women as monstrous in relation to their sexuality and reproductive systems.[4] She is monstrous in a specific way and in a manner that does not apply to the (often sympathetic) male monster of myth, literature, and horror. I developed the term 'monstrous-feminine' to distinguish her from male monsters who were rarely defined, or displayed, in the horror genre in terms of their abject reproductive powers and malleable, leaking bodies. The monstrous-feminine is not a simple reversal of the male monster. Patriarchal ideology argues she is abject by virtue of her very nature. According to Kristeva the fully symbolic body must, 'bear no trace of its debt to nature…it should endure no gash…the sign of belonging to the impure…'[5]

The abject is a construct designed to shore up the power of the group that organises and controls society – its laws, language, religion and ethics. Kristeva defines the abject as that which crosses borders and threatens to undermine society and selfhood. It resides on 'the other side'. Abjection is that which:

> disturbs identity, system, order. What does not respect borders, positions rules. The in-between, the ambiguous, the composite…the shameless rapist…Any crime because it draws attention to the fragility of the law, is abject.[6]

Abjection is not an object *per se* but a process, an undermining, destructive process that attacks the symbolic order. Kristeva argues that bodily wastes are particularly abject because they point to the frailty of the body and its inability to always signify that which is clean and proper. 'Any secretion or discharge, anything that leaks out of the feminine or masculine body defiles'. Patriarchal societies deem women as abject because their reproductive and maternal roles transgress boundaries. Women's bodily fluids (menstrual blood, afterbirth, breast milk) leak, crossing borders from the inside to the outside of the body. Throughout history woman's reproductive body has been seen as unclean or abject and as such subject to various taboos. Toilet training in which the mother cleans up the infant's bodily wastes is also abject by association.

The mother who (s)mothers the infant, particularly the male child, and undermines his attempts to break away and enter the (male) world of law and language is abject because her world, and all it represents, threatens the proper functioning of the patriarchal order by invading its boundaries. Her desires and actions cross a fragile border that must be maintained at all costs. In this sense abjection is relative. If women were to control society and depict men (wanting to re-assert their power) as abject the latter would doubtless be defined in relation to violence and aggression.

Kristeva distinguishes between women who are defined as abject and the abject male. As discussed above, she argues that patriarchal ideology abjects women in relation to their sexual, reproductive and mothering functions while the male is abject in relation to acts of violence and treachery when he threatens to undermine the dominant order by traversing its borders and boundaries. As I discuss in a recent book, *Return of the Monstrous-Feminine: Feminist New Wave Cinema* men are represented as abject in Feminist New Wave cinema overwhelmingly in relation to violence and rape.[7] They live by the rules of what is best described as an 'aggressive phallicity'.[8] What is interesting is that woman's abjection, which offers compelling yet repulsive displays of gendered bodily horror, has an unparalleled power to shock, particularly the male viewer, but also the power to delight the female spectator. A defining characteristic of abjection is that it is ambiguous. We are perversely attracted to abject states of being, precisely because they are forbidden or taboo. When the monstrous-feminine revolts, we cross to 'the other side', drawn by the power of her rage and empathy for her denigration. The journey is confronting but also cathartic.

In the first edition of *The Monstrous-Feminine,* I explored films such as those listed above, that represent the monstrous-feminine as monstrous because she is an abject figure. She is powerful and terrifying but, in the end, she is also *abjected*, that is, she does not control her own narrative. Ideology, however, does not always run smoothly. There are gaps, contradictions and mismatches. In a number of films from this earlier period, such as *Carrie* and *The Brood*, the monstrous-feminine found a way to speak in her own voice before she was silenced by the ending in narratives invariably brought to the screen by male writers and directors. When women claim these stories however, they often take delight in undermining the male symbolic.
It is salient to compare these films with the artworks of Cindy Sherman, a female artist who created her version of the monstrous-feminine from her own, often camp, perspective during the eighties and nineties. Simon Taylor writes, 'Sherman has increasingly produced monstrous representations of the feminine – wearing false breasts, pig snouts, and other prosthetics…'[9] For example, in *Untitled (#187)*1989 she puts a deliberately grotesque pregnant female body on display while in *Untitled (Vagina)* 1992, she transforms the vagina into an uncanny creature. Sherman appears to delight in creating a mocking, disrespectful scary female other/outsider. Her film, *Office Killer*, 1997, similarly revels in being non-symbolic. Female reviewers have stated how satisfying they find scenes that depict the monstrous-feminine's power. In discussing her response to the female alien/femme fatale in *Under the Skin*, Jonathan Glazer, 2014, played by Scarlett Johansson, Kjerstin Johnson explains that to her the Alien's embodiment of an earthly femme fatale was 'deliciously powerful' but her transformation into a 'human woman was uncomfortably familiar.'[10]

A great deal has changed in relation to the monstrous-feminine of horror in the new millennium. In *Return of the Monstrous-Feminine* I explore these changes, specifically the new 'face' of the monstrous-feminine. More women are producing and directing their own horror films, writing new scripts and speaking in their own voices. They have effectively reclaimed the image of the monstrous-feminine in order to tell personal, intimate stories. Stylish and ground-breaking, their films have won major international awards. Many explore gender, queer sensibilities, the rights of women, the earth and social minorities. This new generation of directors include Marina de Van, *In My Skin*, 2002; Karyn Kusama, *Jennifer's Body*, 2009; Jennifer Kent, *The Babadook,* 2014; Ana Lily Amirpour, *A Girl Walks Home Alone at Night*, 2014; Ísold Uggadóttir, *And Breathe Normally*, 2018; Kitty Green, *The Assistant*, 2019; Emerald Fennell, *Promising Young Woman*, 2020; Chloé Zhao, *Nomadland*, 2020; and Julia Ducournau, *Titane*, 2021. The monstrous-feminine of these texts, is represented as having a different relationship to abjection. She undertakes a personal journey into the dark night of abjection where she comes to understand that her sexual desire and reproductive body are not *per se* abject. Those aspects of women's lives and bodies that were once abjected as a source of horror (blood, birth, animality) along with a desire to use violence to redress acts of male aggression are no longer represented as abject in a negative sense. To some this realisation inspires rage – a rage that she unleashes on her adversaries as in *Ginger Snaps*, *Jennifer's Body*, *Revenge*, *The Nightingale*, *Spoor* and *Promising Young Woman*. The feminist chador-clad vampire of *A Girl Walks Home Alone at Night* singles out violent men as her victims; she has a mission, as well as a hunger, to fulfill. It is difficult not to relate her acts of retribution to the oppression of women in extremist religious theocracies as well as democratic patriarchal societies. These texts have become part of a new wave of feminist filmmaking designed to undercut misogynistic stereotypes of the monstrous-feminine and undermine the masculine symbolic order. *Return of the Monstrous-Feminine* argues that woman has become the *subject* of her own revolt, not just in horror films, but also films which explore the horror of the everyday. She draws on abjection, which I call radical abjection, to fuel her revolt and create a new culture and language.

Kristeva argues that abjection can also lead to transformation: 'In abjection, revolt is completely within being. Within the being of language…the subject of abjection is eminently productive of culture'.[11] In *Revolt She Said* Kristeva states that what is now important, post-1968, is not large-scale political and social revolutions, which in a sense failed, but 'intimate revolt', that is, a questioning of one's own being instead of the (male) preference for pedantic quibbling.

> The arrival of women at the forefront of the social and ethical scene has had the result of revalorizing the sensory experience, the antidote to technical hair-splitting.[12]

Kristeva sees literature as one of the most productive forms in which to present such a revolt. I argue that film and visual media also offer productive terrains with which to explore intimate revolt and the female protagonist's changed relationship to abjection.

A central aim of *Return of the Monstrous-Feminine* is to discuss the emergence of what I have termed 'feminist new wave cinema'. I argue that this new wave of horror is intergeneric, political and focuses on the monstrous-feminine, not as an object, but as a subject of her own narrative, speaking in her own voice. In all the films mentioned above, the female protagonist immerses herself in an act of intimate revolt as she travels into the dark night of abjection to question her own being. In particular, she is in revolt against male violence and an oppressive social order. Feminist directors appear to be drawn to intergeneric forms, mixing horror with other genres such as the road movie, lesbian drama, and rape–revenge film. Genre boundaries are blurred in these original and daring films, as award-winning Polish director Agnieszka Holland says of her film, *Spoor*, 2017, about an elderly retired engineer who takes revenge on those who harm and kill animals:

> You cannot really tell if it is a thriller, a dark comedy, some kind of ecological manifesto, an artistic drama, or perhaps a fairy tale. It's a mix of reality and fantasy, and the main character is some kind of witch from my generation who just cannot accept the cruelty and the injustice of this male-driven hunting chorus.[13]

Directors are also focussed on films about the horror of the everyday. In this respect, I have argued that ordinary women who reject the proper feminine role (Kimberly Peirce's *Boys Don't Cry* 1999; Tod Haynes' *Carol* 2015; Celine Emerald Fennell's *Promising Young Woman* 2010; Lee Daniel's *The United States vs. Billie Holiday* 2021) and experience the horror of the everyday are also seen as monstrous in terms of patriarchal values. In Emerald Fennell's *Promising Young Woman* the heroine deliberately feigns drunkenness, putting herself on sexual display to tempt predatory young men to take advantage of her at which point she drops her masquerade and verbally attacks them for their abject behaviour. Such women do not conform to the acceptable modes of femininity; they have rejected the 'proper' female role and as such eroded the boundaries of the male symbolic order. I focus on films mainly directed by women, but also by men, in the new millennium. I argue that these directors have been inspired by new theoretical developments and various social justice movements such as #MeToo, Black Lives Matter and Extinction-Rebellion. They represent the monstrous-feminine as on a journey into abjection during which she challenges the male symbolic order of law and language and from which she emerges changed, even transformed.

In the recently published second edition of the original *The Monstrous-Feminine*, I have included a new section on the monstrous-feminine as nonhuman.[14] Like the monstrous-feminine of feminist new wave horror, she is also in a different relationship to abjection compared to her earlier counterparts. I have called this 'radical abjection'. Here I explore the representation of the monstrous-feminine as nonhuman – animal, sentient zombie, alien, plant, and other. This new section is informed by a recent theoretical development – the turn to nonhuman theory in the humanities and social sciences. The monstrous-feminine questions not just the anthropocentrism of the patriarchal order but also the so-called uniqueness of the human. Embracing the nonhuman through an often-horrific journey into the dark night of abjection is represented in many of these films as a liberating act.

The timeliness of this international exhibition, *From the other side*, speaks to the significance of the changes currently taking place in artistic practices that address the power of horror to enable women to explore their innermost fears, fantasies, and desires. These changes, I argue in *Return of the Monstrous-Feminine* constitute a new wave of feminist artistic practice in film and the visual arts. The monstrous-feminine, as an artistic and mythic concept, offers the possibility of transformation and liberation. Her great strength is her abject monstrousness which she weaponizes in order to undermine oppressive social and political structures which Jacques Derrida sees as held together by 'phallogocentrism',[15] that is, the privileging of the phallus in the creation of society which leads to the oppression of women and minorities. The monstrous-feminine has no fear of the phallus and all that it signifies. She fascinates, repels and revolutionises; it is a sign of her success that her outrageous behaviour is deliciously satisfying.

1. Barbara Creed, 'Horror and the Monstrous-Feminine: An Imaginary Abjection', *Screen,* volume 27, issue 1, 1986. pp.44-70.
2. The original *Screen* article has been translated into various languages including Japanese, Korean, Spanish, Hungarian and Russian. There has been strong interest in Asian countries. See: Raechel Dumas, *The Monstrous-Feminine in Contemporary Japanese Popular Culture*, Palgrave Macmillan, London, New York, Shanghai, 2018; and Hunju Lee, 'Transformations of the Monstrous Feminine in the New Asian Female Ghost Films' in *Diogenes*, Volume 62, Issue 1, 2017. Google notes there are over 2.7 million entries online referring to the monstrous-feminine.
3. Barbara Creed, *The Monstrous-Feminine: Film, Feminism, Psychoanalysis*, Routledge, London, New York, 1993.
4. Julia Kristeva, *Powers of Horror: An Essay on Abjection*, trans. Leon S. Roudiez, Columbia University Press, New York, 1982.
5. Ibid. p.102.
6. Ibid. p.4.
7. Barbara Creed, *Return of the Monstrous-Feminine: Feminist New Wave Cinema*, Routledge, New York, 2022.
8. Ibid. p.8.
9. Simon Taylor, 'The Phobic Object: Abjection in Contemporary Art', *Abject Art: Repulsion and Desire in American Art*, Whitney Museum of American Art, Whitney Independent Study Program, New York, 1993. p.62.
10. Kjerstin Johnson, 'The Two Halves of "Under the Skin', *Bitch Media*, 9 June, 2014, https://www.bitchmedia.org/post/under-the-skin-review-feminism-scarlett-johansson.
11. Julia Kristeva, *Powers of Horror: An Essay on Abjection*. p.45.
12. Julia Kristeva, *Revolt, She Said*, ed. Sylvère Lotringer, trans. Brian O'Keefe, Semiotext(e), Los Angeles, 2002. p.5.
13. Agnieszka Holland, 'An Interview with *Spoor* Director Agnieszka Holland', interview by Cynthia Biret. *Riot Material*, 16 January, 2018, https://www.riotmaterial.com/interview-with-spoor-director-agnieszka-holland/
14. Barbara Creed, *The Monstrous-Feminine: Film, Feminism, Psychoanalysis*, second edition, Routledge, London, New York, 2024.
15. Jacques, Derrida, '"Eating Well," or the Calculation of the Subject: An Interview with Jacques Derrida', *Who Comes After the Subject?*, eds. Eduardo Cadava, Peter Connor, and Jean-Luc Nancy, Routledge, New York, 1991. p.96-119.

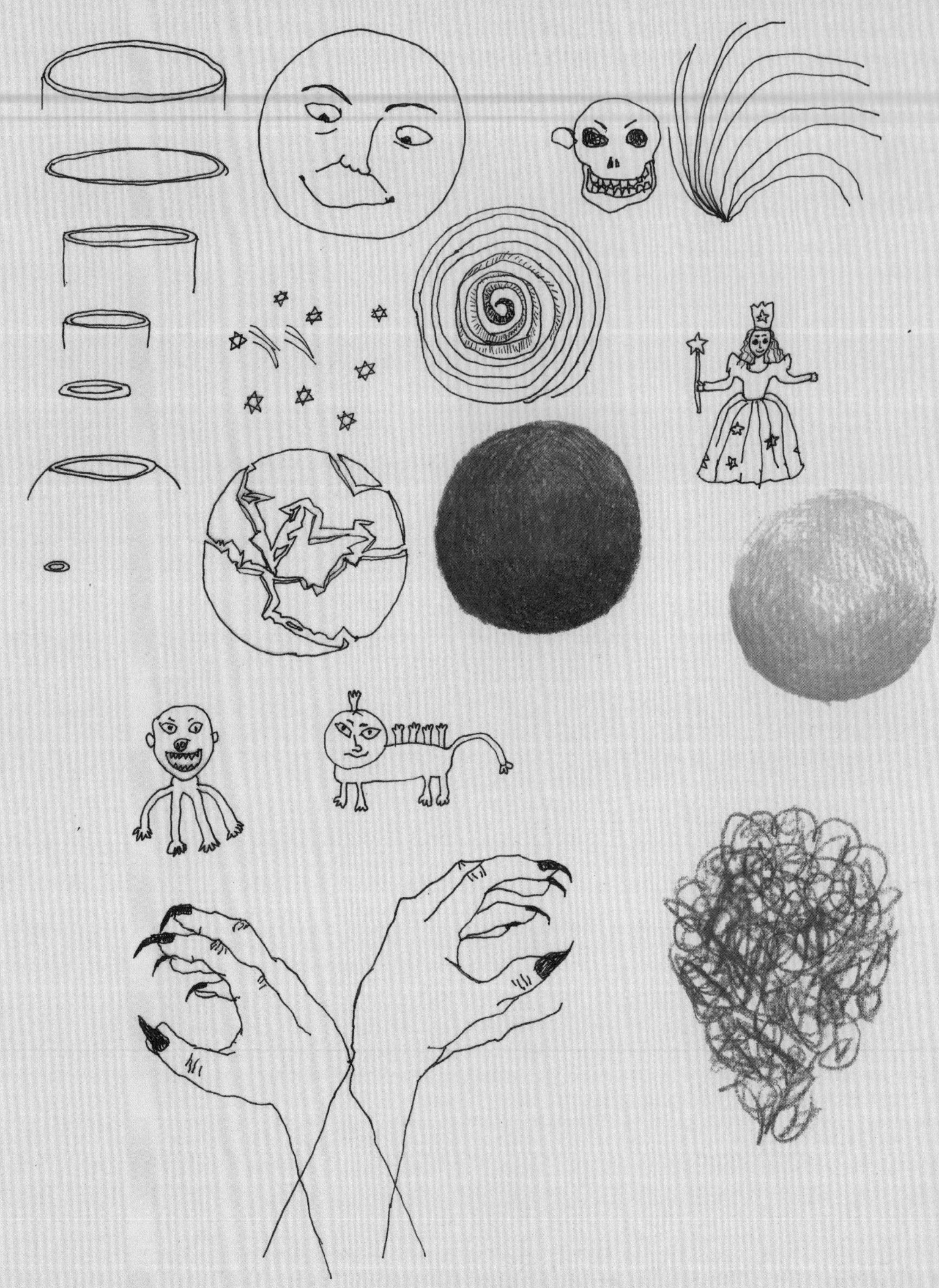

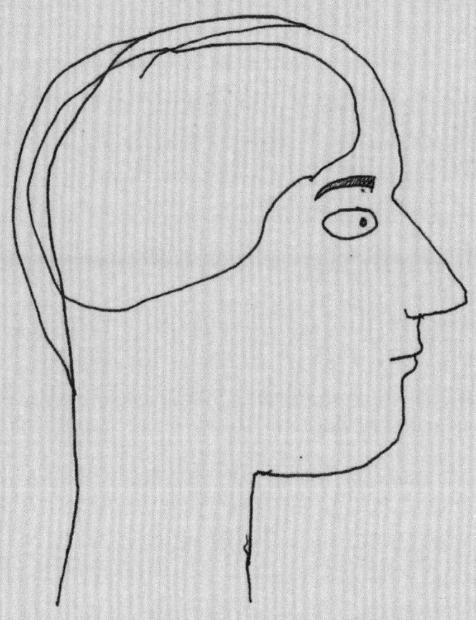

Love

Fear

Birth
Death
Angel
Devil

Danger
Disgrace

That Which Crushes Us

Elyse Goldfinch

It begins with the eye.

The eye is one of the most indelible symbols in cinema - from the sliced eyeball of Luis Buñuel and Salvador Dalí's *Un Chien Andalou* 1929, to the Oedipal blinding of Michael Powell's *Peeping Tom*, 1960; from the climax of Bob Clark's *Black Christmas* 1974 where the killer's bulging eye is seen staring at his next victim through a tiny crack in the door, to the demonic skull with a single intact eyeball dug up from a freshly ploughed furrow in Piers Haggard's *The Blood on Satan's Claw* 1971. In horror films, the eye variously represents fear, subliminal desire, the violence of spectatorship, and castration anxieties.[1] Monstrous-feminine beings – including Medusa, the Gorgon and the Siren – use the eye as a shield to violently threaten and destroy the patriarchal gaze.[2]

Eyes are also an ongoing motif of protection, intimacy and mourning for artist Heather B Swann whose work *Never Let Me Go* 2023 hangs like a porous veil at the threshold of both entrances to *From the other side*. Made from hundreds of linen eyelashes to form a spiderweb-like pattern, the audience is invited to make physical contact with the work as they enter. The itchy sensation of eyelashes gently passing over skin induces a tactile, bodily sensation that separates the outside world from the imaginary enclosure of the exhibition beyond.

The eye continues in Swann's *Human Frailty* 2023, featuring thirteen miniature reliquaries containing disembodied crying eyes, held safely within wooden pods, and made sorrowful with crystal tears. There's a deep longing in these fragments of lost souls left to weep their tragic demise into eternity. In a third sculpture in the ensemble, *The Three Sisters* 2023, Swann creates a haunting mise-en-scene featuring two women, presumably sisters, atop three uncannily elongated beds. The third figure is absent, her bed empty, anticipating her possible return. Replacing the sisters' nipples with eyes, Swann subverts the passivity of the classical female nude, returning the audience's voyeuristic gaze with their own unblinking, monstrous vision.

The psychological space of the domestic is a long-running theme for French-American artist Louise Bourgeois, our Grande Dame Guignol of the exhibition.[3] Bourgeois' strange, surreal, sometimes horrific imagery repeatedly reveals the hidden violence and suppression located within the home, particularly from the lens of childhood. In her iconic work *Spider* 1995, Bourgeois references the abject maternal figure, a mother so frightening and monstrous she is often depicted as gargantuan, looming over her audience. Bourgeois claims the mother in the form of the spider to fiercely protect her child from external threats.[4] Similarly in *Untitled (safety pins)* 1991, Bourgeois considers the safety pin as an object that can mend and support, but at the same time can pierce and cause harm. In *Arched Figure* 1993, suspended before a naked male torso, a woman's body is contorted to its extreme as she is bowed in agony, extasy or demonic splendour, her expression hysterical and mouth agape. All three works play with the contradictory emotions of protection and terror, power and impotence.

Berlin-based artist, Marianna Simnett also interrogates the binary categorisation of the nuclear family in *The Udder* 2014. Set on a dairy farm in West Sussex, the film's protagonist Isabel is an archetype of childhood innocence who longs to delay her impending puberty, begging to 'stay clean'.[5] In the muddy fields she discovers a scalpel which she contemplates using to slice off her nose, a reference to the expression, to 'cut off one's nose to spite your face', based on the story of Saint Æbba the Younger who disfigured her face to avoid being raped by Vikings in the ninth century. Author Kathy Acker presents the tension between purity and the threat of contamination in her book *My Mother: Demonology*, 1995, when she quotes her father, 'in order for me to paint horror, I have to see the horror in myself... I must violate both vision and my own child'.[6] The scalpel is later seen dissecting an udder infected with mastitis, a substitute for the absence of violence. Disconnected from the animal, the udder is an organ without a body, equally violated and violating.

While Simnett references fables with grotesque imagery, artist Clare Milledge is occupied by magical, folkloric and shamanistic approaches to forge profound connections between the human and non-human. In her work *Badb: bro im glitched* 2023, Milledge references The Mórrígan, a warrior queen from Irish-Celtic mythology often considered the guardian of the dead who was a transporter between life and the underworld. Originally considered a healer and protector of the land, she was recognised for shapeshifting into the form of a crow, known as a *Babd*. However, her image also shifted, and she was later described as the 'harbinger of doom', inciting fear and confusion, becoming more monstrous with every retelling.[7] Alongside historical references, Milledge's title references online gaming speak; 'bro, I'm glitched' is a phrase used when a virtual character malfunctions, speaking to the ways technology can corrupt the subconscious construction of the self.

Both Naomi Blacklock and Cybele Cox directly reference the image of the witch. Blacklock employs voice, breath and ritualised sounds and objects to address the cultural significance of the witch as an, 'emancipatory symbol for alterity in contemporary art'.[8] *Breath Hovering Beneath the Base* 2016/23 is a single-channel sound installation featuring the artist breathing rhythmically into a microphone. Her breath becomes increasingly distorted above a relentless and unsettling base drone. Occasionally her breathing escalates to aural screaming as the intensity and tension in the work builds, releasing the work from its hypnotic state. Blacklock claims her use of screaming is 'deeply rooted in a desperate desire to locate an inclusive and intersectional female experience',[9] particularly as an expression for self-determination, freedom and revolt.

In *The Monstrous-Feminine,* 1993, Barbara Creed suggests 'there is one incontestably monstrous role in the horror film that belongs to woman – that of the witch.'[10] The witch in horror is typically foregrounded by her dangerous sexuality and threat to the patriarchal symbolic order.[11] Cybele Cox's life-size ceramic witch, *The Hag* 2023, sensually emerges as if from the belly of hell. On all fours in a 'birthing position', she is painted entirely in an earthy red, adorned by luscious gold jewellery draped across her torso and wrist. Cox's 'hag' combines exaggerated female and male physical characteristics: broad shoulders, pendulous breasts, protruding veins, tiny feet. In doing so, she defies typical witch-like characterisations. Mirroring the woman in Bourgeois' *Arched Figure*, her mouth hangs open just inches away from a snake slithering around her raised arm, perhaps inviting it inside. Across cultures and religions, the origin of women's so-called deception against men is often cast back to her kinship to snakes.[12] Absorbed in her hypnotic state, Cox's witch fixates on this ritual task, fiercely embracing her supposed monstrousness.

Artist Kellie Wells' practice engages magic and the occult as a symbol for exploring disobedience and emancipation, as well as the subjective representation of the self, often foregrounding her own body or subjectivity within the work. Raised in a strictly Catholic household, her large-scale photograph *Through Catherine* 2019 reflects on a memory of one of the nuns at her religious school. The photograph presents the artist masquerading as the nun who haunts her childhood memories, a figure for whom she feels conflicted fear and empathy. The artist's face is obscured, barely visible behind the light that surrounds it, almost possessed within this character. The void where her face should appear becomes a portal into a new space of perception. Five hanging bronze sculptures accompany the photographic image, depicting archetypal women. Also described by the artist as portals or doorways each sculpture bears the unique shape of a sigil, a symbol used in magic that represents a desire to disrupt and reform how women exist through history in our imagination as much as our reality.

New York-based artist Theron Debris also deploys himself as the subject of seven large photographic prints. Juxtaposed between hyper-coloured pop and gothic black and white, the works depict images of the artist from online dating and dom profiles, with his body heavily manipulated, turned inside out, as if on the precipice of dissolution. In some images the artist's features are still recognisable, in others they morph into highly evocative central core imagery, a suggestive fusion of desire and monstrousness. In her 2011 book *The Art of Cruelty*, author Maggie Nelson draws a potent connection between the language of horror and pornographic films, singling out the term 'meat' to describe both genres' obsession with exposing, exploiting and fragmenting the body into an unflinching spectacle of flesh.[13] Theorist Julia Kristeva also notes that pleasure might be experienced in proximity to horror – arousal and horror coincide to distort the 'language of want, of fear that edges up to it and runs along its edges',[14] later describing, 'the sublime point at which the abject collapses in a burst of beauty that overwhelms us – and that cancels our existence'.[15] The abjection in Debris's photographs becomes a place of devastating beauty, of potentiality beyond the fetishised 'meat' of the body.

Like Debris's images, Christchurch-based artist Lonnie Hutchinson's drawings are in states of transformation - fluid, porous, leaking. Hutchinson's work references her cultural heritage (Ngāti kuri ki Ngāi Tahu, Samoan, Celtic), commenting on ancient traditions and fusing the personal and political to critique the violent effects of colonisation. In *From the other side* Hutchinson presents three drawings depicting figures that defy categories of gender. Her raw and unrestrained application of ink allows the bodies beginning to morph and lose shape, to become fluid. As art historian Linda Tyler describes, 'Hutchinson shows the body's sexual characteristics to be provisionally constructed… reinforcing the sketchiness of gender identity, and the impulse to change'.[16] Horror also explores the body in a state of transition through an ontological negotiation between gender, sexuality, identity and desire. Their ability to shapeshift underpins their capacity to traverse and resist imperial classification.

Maria Kozic's *Calendar Girls* 1999 also deal with seduction and horror in her suite of twelve large-scale paintings presenting pulpy depictions of archetypal 'final girls',[17] a trope coined by Carol J Clover to describe the sole female survivor in slasher films of the 1970s, 80s and 90s. Over this time, the final girl was typically depicted as virginal or sexually unavailable, avoiding many of the vices favoured by her teenage peers like alcohol and drugs. She followed a formula of purity and virtue that ensured her survival, but as Clover argues, according to rules set and upheld by patriarchal standards. Other female characters must be punished and experience abject terror to be purged of their pursuit of personal pleasure.[18] If horror films of this era expressed female desire, it was only to demonstrate its monstrosity.

Kozic's protagonists typify the beauty standards of the classic final girl – thin, pretty and white –upon closer inspection their features unravel to reveal something far more menacing – scars and tattoos, slashed skin and barbed wire hair. All appear to be survivors of various unspoken horrors and yet they emerge defiantly from the canvas, uncompromising, even seductive, as they return the viewer's gaze. To not only survive, but to defy victimhood, they become gloriously rebellious, vengeful and abject.

From Swann's *Three Sisters* to Kozic's *Calendar Girls*, the artists in *From the other side* represent their so-called 'otherness' through what Creed terms 'figures in revolt.'[19] These figures legitimise lingering and unrestrained feelings of anger, defiance, lust, and compulsion.[20] In horror, women, queer, trans and non-binary subjectivities come together as 'a solidarity of the monsters',[21] in order to be liberated. As Kristeva argues, the abject is that which 'crushes'[22] us. We must be crushed in order to confront our true selves, embrace our monstrousness, and preserve our power.

1. Barbara Creed lists three main categories of Freud's theory of the uncanny including, 'castration anxieties expressed as a fear of the female genitals or of dismembered limbs, a severed head or hand, loss of the eyes, fear of going blind'. See: Barbara Creed, *The Monstrous Feminine: Film Feminism and Psychoanalysis*, Routledge, London and New York, 1993, p. 53.
2. Ibid, p. 2.
3. The Grande Dame Guignol is a term recently reclaimed by horror film makers and critics to subvert insulting terms such as the hag and the crone. The Grande Dame Guignol is now celebrated for embracing her power and rejecting the assumed subservience of aging women. See: Anna Bogutskaya, 'Sunset Boulevard', *The Final Girls*, podcast, released 10 November 2023, https://thefinalgirlspodcast.transistor.fm/s6/1.
4. Deborah Wye and Carol Smith, *The Prints of Louise Bourgeois*, The Museum of Modern Art, New York, 1994, p. 113.
5. Marianna Simnett, The Udder, 2014.
6. Kathy Acker, *My Mother: Demonology*, Grove Press, New York, 1993, p. 98.
7. Chris Thompson and Isolde Carmody, 'Encountering the Mórrígan', *Story Archaeology*, podcast, released 15 June 2016, https://storyarchaeology.com/series-5episode-6-encountering-the-morrigan/.
8. Naomi Blacklock, *Conjuring Alterity: Refiguring The Witch and The Female Scream in Contemporary Art*, Queensland University of Technology, Brisbane, 2019, p. ii.
9. Ibid p.2.
10. Barbara Creed, *The Monstrous Feminine*, 1993, p. 73.
11. Ibid, p. 76.
12. Alongside the religious stories that link women, snakes and evil, there is also an historical connection with menstruation, as Creed notes: 'Some ancient cultures associated the full moon and woman's monthly bleeding with the snake. All three – the moon, snake and woman's cycle – move through stages in which the old is shed and the new reborn'. Ibid, p. 64.
13. Maggie Nelson, *The Art of Cruelty: A Reckoning*, W. W. Norton, New York and London, 2011, p. 181.
14. Julia Kristeva, 'Something to be scared of', *Powers of Horror: An Essay on Abjection*, Columbia University Press, New York, p. 38.
15. Julia Kristeva, *Powers of Horror*, p. 210.
16. Linda Tyler, *Body Narratives: nudes by Lonnie Hutchinson*, Ramp Gallery, Hamilton City, 2016.
17. Carol J Clover, 'Her Body Himself', *Men, Women and Chainsaws: Gender in the Modern Horror Film*,

Princeton University Press, New Jersey, 1992, p. 35.
18. Ibid, p. 36.
19. Barbara Creed, 'Introduction', *Return of the Monstrous-Feminine: Feminist New Wave Cinema*, Routledge, London and New York, 2022, p.2.
20. Andrea Juno and V. Vale (eds), 'Angry Women', *Re/Search*, 1991, p. 5.
21. Jack Halbastam, in Paul B. Preciado, *Can The Monster Speak?*, Fitzcarraldo Editions, London, 2021, p. iii.
22. Julia Kristeva, *Powers of Horror*, p. 2.

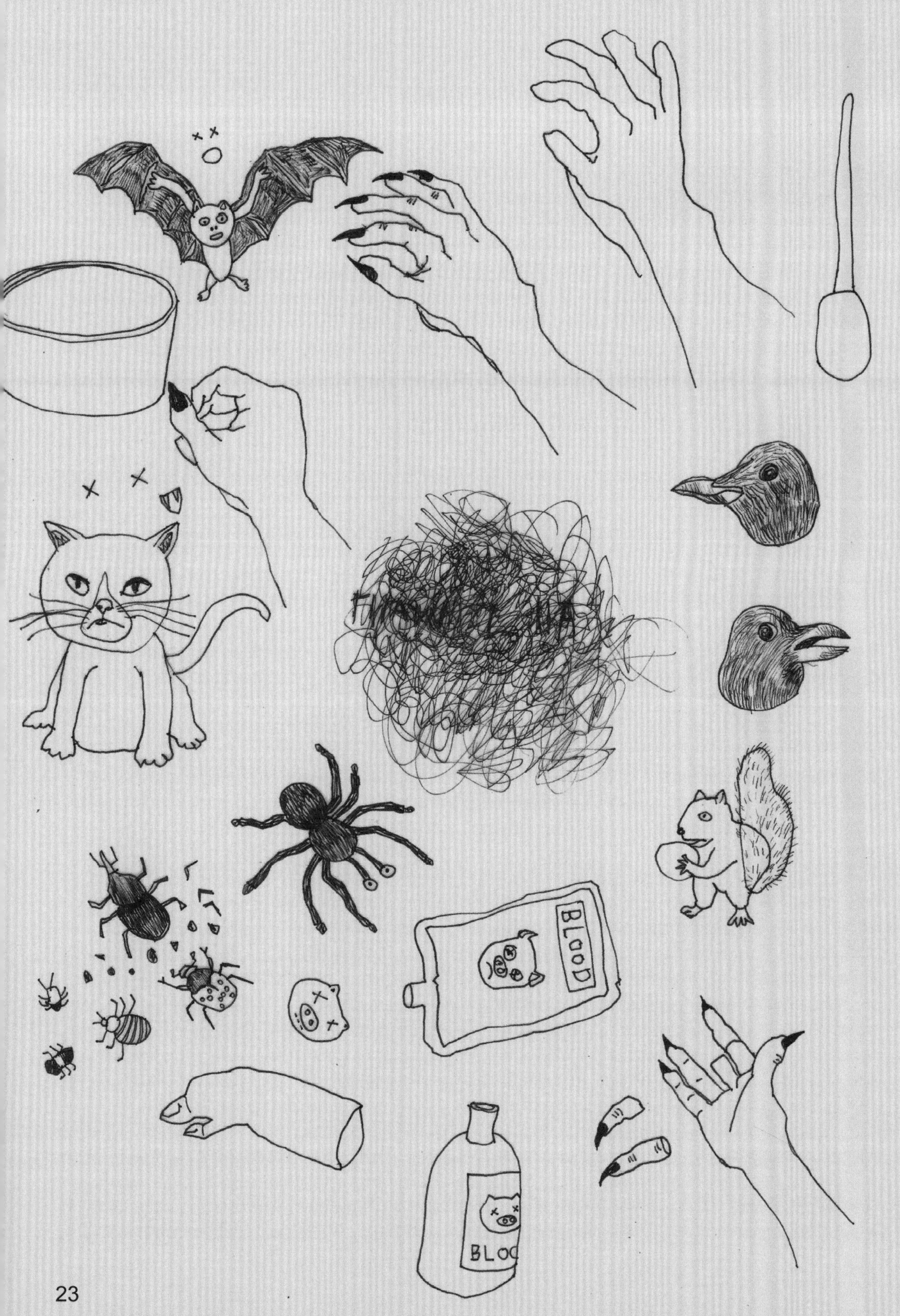
BLOOD

Power in Difference
Jessica Clark

> Her monstrousness is a force for change.[1]

From the other side embraces horror as a necessary and cathartic release. With a sixth mass extinction underway in tandem with an unprecedented climate crisis, the suggestion of progress is becoming more and more of a farce. The future is uncertain. War, violence, abuses of power – the pressure builds. The existential threat of the current moment is very real, from every angle – social, political, personal, cultural, and environmental. This threat is tenfold for those considered other – women, First Nations communities, people of colour, and gender diverse communities; those that challenge the patriarchal and symbolic order. Even though humanity is more connected than ever, there is a growing disconnection between people, place and space. Moreover, misinformation is thriving, and human ignorance is seemingly at an all-time high. The anxiety and fear in the air grows thicker and thicker, day-in-day-out; fiction reflects reality and reality reflects fiction.

> The world has become a place full of fears that control us, that hover like dark clouds every day. We have never been closer to the end.[2]

In times of crisis – historically and in the now – horror thrives, providing a distraction from the real, 'a chance' to face fear.[3] In dialogue with the current reclamation and resurgence of horror, in feminist new wave cinema in particular*, From the other side* stages a revolt that is both political and personal. Through a curatorial framework that centres academic Barbara Creed's idea of the monstrous-feminine as 'a force for change',[4] the exhibition channels notions of revenge, rage, revolt and protection. As articulated by Creed, the lens of the monstrous-feminine conveys horror as an 'emotional force' and 'artistic aesthetic' that speaks for the rights of women and social minorities.[5] Equally, the exhibition harnesses the capacity for horror to transgress and destabilise perceived forms power.[6] With the intention to inspire new ways of thinking, seeing and being in the world, *From the other side* invites the viewer to consider reality from a multitude of perspectives, beyond oneself and what is known.

A journey into the underworld of the human psyche unfolds in Suzan Pitt's surreal and strange animation *Visitation* 2011. Prompted by a lived experience, of working alone in an isolated cabin in the woods, Pitt's film navigates a series of inter-connected and unnerving 'worst case scenarios' of psychological chaos and torment. A heavenly hell of unending life and death are in tandem with the alternating intensity of the narrator and musical score, and the silence in-between. Pitt's protagonists are intensely sinister and dark, inflicting horrifying acts of violence that emphasise mortality, and the existential threat of depression and paranoia. *Visitation* conveys psychological distress, shock and fear, drawing attention to the susceptibility of the mind, the threat of the self, and the idea that death is not necessarily the end.

Mia Boe's digitally manipulated prints, *A Desolate Primitive Place* and *I Suspect*, both 2023, are derived from two quintessentially Australian films: *Wake in Fright*, 1971, and *Walkabout,* 1971. Each work manipulates an unnerving and ambiguous scene from these classic films that convey the encroachment of the built environment and a frightening disconnection between people and place. Boe interrupts each scene with a strategically positioned self-portrait, inserting herself as a means to reclaim space, return the gaze, and reassert presence. Shown side-by-side, *A Desolate Primitive Place* and *I Suspect* offer uncomfortable and unembellished reflections on Australian society – both past and present – emphasising notions of alienation and racism, 'profanity spawned by fear'[7] of the other.

Julia Robinson's sculptural 'scarecrows' – *Double Stumps*, *The Pledge*, *Burrow Mump*, *Tatterdmalion* 2021-2022, from her recent series *The Beckoning Blade* – awaken ghosts buried deep within the soil. Each sculptural assemblage presents a splayed smock garment handmade and hand-dyed by the artist, propped or framed by a repurposed and modified scythe; a tool used to reap or harvest crops, and a symbol of death. Grounded in the struggle for survival on the land, *The Beckoning Blade* series conjures notions of cult and myth, decay and renewal, and the fine line between a love and fear of nature. Together, the works materialise as a suite of frightening figures that embrace the role of harbinger and set the stage for sacrifice.

In Tracey Moffatt's *A Haunting* 2021-2023, a dilapidated weatherboard house appears at dusk, isolated in the landscape and intermittently illuminated with a deep red light; a pulse, like a heartbeat.[8] Projected at large scale, the house repeatedly emerges and disappears in rhythm with the viewer's breath, while the overlaid chorus of crickets generate a heightened sense of unease; what might be hidden in the darkness, what might be revealed by the light? *A Haunting* continues to cycle, almost endlessly, withholding explicit shock or reveal, and prolonging the threshold between day and night. Moffatt has explained the work can be read as a 'crime scene',[9] enacting a vigil to colonial and gendered violence, most of which goes unseen, but the home and the earth bear witness.

In Australia, violence against women is 'disturbingly common', ranking eighth for rates of domestic violence among G20 Nations.[10] On average, one woman a week is murdered by a current or former partner.[11] Further, Aboriginal and Torres Strait Islander women are even more likely to be subjected to physical and sexual violence.[12] Karla Dickens' *Warrior Woman IV*, *VI,* and *XIV* 2017 present a series of metallic-sculptures – underpants – adorned with a range of charged materials and found objects assembled to serve as a warning. The *Warrior Women* are armed and ready for the fight, transforming everyday detritus into empowering symbols for protection and empowerment. Dickens' entwines sorrow with wry humour to express the rage in the face of horrifying stories and statistics that make explicit the past and present forms of gendered and racist violence – sexual, physical, emotional and economic – against women, and First Nations women in particular, in this country and beyond.

Sometimes the only way through is within. Minyoung Kim conjures dark forces and fantasies as a means of navigating the uncertainty of emotional experience, through a selection of darkly humorous pastel drawings and hand-drawn stop-motion animations. Employing a 'creepy-cute' aesthetic, in the artist's words, Kim's animated *Live Drawing Books I-III* 2018 concoct a range of spells and potions through recurring motifs, emblems and characters. Her drawings *Staring*, *The Bath, The Grass,* and *The Night,* all 2021, depict black cats, bloody bodies, and staring eyes, lifting the veil on her inner-most feelings, ones that language fails to express, which are hidden deep within the subconscious, superstition, and revealed through introspection of the self.

Stifled forces – Constantly Swelling. Will the Levee break? 2023 by Jemima Lucas features a large metal rod that violently punctures the gallery wall, creating a dramatic rupture in the white cube. The rod is connected to a series of wire cables that expand the installation outward, traversing space and affixing themselves to multiple walls at varying angles. At the point where the wires meet, a severed and disembodied ox tongue cast in bronze is offered-up, suggesting sacrifice. The object is hostile and unnerving, staged in relation to an excavator bucket that doubles as a cauldron; filled to the brim with bubbling, deep green engine coolant. Lucas' materiality functions as bodily conduits, snagged by insurmountable pressure, triggering a visceral unease, an ambiguious threat to survival. Through relationality and repulsion, *Stifled forces – Constantly Swelling. Will the Levee Break?* generates an ecology of prolonged tension, structural instability, and potential violence.

Naomi Kantjuriny's suite of twelve ink drawings collectively titled *Mamu (Good Spirits)* 2023 depict a swarm of mamu spirits delicately rendered in ghostly white ink on black paper. Mamu are night-dwelling spirits that bridge the physical and ancestral realm and interfere with the living in both good and bad ways. While mostly mischievous, Kantjuriny has depicted 'good' mamu, the spirits that work concurrently with the artist's Ngangkari (traditional healing) practice. *Mamu (Good Spirits)* speaks to the vulnerability of the human spirit, of physical and emotional health, and the importance of protection; of finding the light and defying the darkness. Kantjuriny explains, 'the good mamu will look after you when you are travelling. They come in different forms and with varying powers.'[13]

A sculptural community of severed hands crawl and sprawl across a two-pronged upholstered staircase to form Zamara Zamara's *Ceramic Gestures* 2019-23. Each hand is exaggerated in form and adorned with long talons that signal gestures ranging from 'peace' to 'get fucked'. As protective 'gestures', they acknowledge that the creation of space sometimes requires defence, particularly for those othered by the social order. Together, they speak to the ways in which communities come together and organise for safety, collective resistance, and to combat fear and hold space for vulnerability. Additionally, Zamara's installation *Like Pulling Teeth* 2023 presents a mouthful of ceramic teeth. Each has a screw driven violently through their centre to convey a seemingly cyclical threat of bodily violence. Together, Zamara's *Ceramic Gestures* and *Like Pulling Teeth* navigate a slippage between human and animal, beautiful and beastly, suggesting power in difference.

As feminist psychoanalyst Julia Kristeva explains, 'Revolt is not simply about rejection and destruction; it is also about starting over. Unlike the word "violence", "revolt" foregrounds an element of renewal and regeneration'[14] – offering-up opportunities for transformation, the unapologetic expansion of self, and rebirth. Through the lens of the monstrous-feminine, *From the other side* stages an empowering revolt that embraces the abject; that which patriarchal society views as threat, that which disturbs 'identity, system, order… [and] does not respect borders, positions, rules.'[15] Collectively, the works scream back at patriarchy, coloniality, and gendered violence, and the threat of the real. *From the other side* invites a reckoning that calls for social and environmental justice, and the agency and empowerment of the other with renewed resolve and collective strength.

1. Barbara Creed, *Return of The Monstrous-Feminine: Feminist New Wave Cinema*, Routledge, London and New York, 2022, p. 4.
2. Guillermo del Toro in Gregorio Belinchón, 'The new horror: Nothing is as scary as reality,' *EL PAÍS,* 1 November 2022, https://english.elpais.com/culture/2022-11-01/the-new-horror-nothing-scares-us-as-much-as-reality.html.
3. Gregorio Belinchón, 'The new horror: Nothing is as scary as reality,' 1 November 2022.
4. Barbara Creed, *Return of The Monstrous-Feminine*, p. 4.
5. Barbara Creed, *The Monstrous-Feminine: Film, Feminism and Psychoanalysis,* Routledge, London and New York, 1993, p. 1.
6. Such as extractive capitalism, colonialism, racism, sexism, misogyny and homophobia.
7. Quote from *Wake in Fright*, Ted Kotcheff, 1971.
8. The house featured in Tracey Moffatt's *A Haunting* 2021-2023 is located on Castlereagh highway (31°27'01.8"S 148°30'27.3"E) just outside Armatree, New South Wales, within Wailwan Country – lighting up on dusk every day until the end of 2023. See: https://www.ahaunting.com.au.
9. Tracey Moffatt, 'Artist Statement', *A Haunting*, https://www.ahaunting.com.au/.
10. Frances Mao, 'How dangerous is Australia for women?', *BBC News*, 22 January 2019, https://www.bbc.com/news/world-australia-46913913#.
11. 'Our Watch Home: Quick Facts', *Our Watch*, 2023, https://www.ourwatch.org.au/quick-facts/.
12. Ibid.
13. Naomi Kantjuriny, Artist Statement, prepared for *From the other side,* Australian Centre for Contemporary Art, 2023.
14. Julia Kristeva, *Revolt She Said*, Semiotext(e), Paris, 2002, p. 123
15. Julia Kristeva in Barbara Creed, *The Monstrous-Feminine*, p. 8.

Image Credits

p. 3	Louise Bourgeois, *Spider* 1995, drypoint on paper, 54.0 x 40.3 cm. © The Easton Foundation. Licensed by Copyright Agency, Sydney. Photo: Christopher Burke.
p. 5	Cybele Cox, *Goat Head* 2017. Photo: Jessica Maurer.
p. 7-23	Minyoung Kim, *Live Drawing Books I-III* 2018 (stills)
p. 29	Heather B Swann, *The Three Sisters* 2023 (detail). Photo: Peter Whyte.
p. 30-31	Heather B Swann, *The Three Sisters* 2023 (detail). Photo: Peter Whyte.
p. 32-33	Louise Bourgeois, *Arched Figure* 1993, drypoint on paper, 39.7 x 55.9 cm. © The Easton Foundation. Licensed by Copyright Agency, Sydney. Photo: Christopher Burke.
p. 34-35	Louise Bourgeois, *Untitled* (*Safety Pins)* 1991, drypoint on paper, 49.4 x 56.0 cm. © The Easton Foundation. Licensed by Copyright Agency, Sydney. Photo: Christopher Burke.
p. 36-37	Cybele Cox, *The Hag* 2023, installation view, Ngununggula, Southern Highlands. Photo: Document Photography.
p. 38	Karla Dickens, *Warrior Woman IV* 2017
p. 39	Karla Dickens, *Warrior Woman XIV* 2017
p. 40	Lonnie Hutchinson, *Justice* 2016, installation view, Ramp Gallery, Hamilton Central.
p. 41	Lonnie Hutchinson, *Equality* 2016, installation view, Ramp Gallery, Hamilton Central.
p. 42-43	Maria Kozic, *Miss December* 1999
p. 44-45	Naomi Blacklock *Body of Voice* 2017, installation view, Metro Arts, Brisbane. Photo: Callum Mcgrath.
p. 46-47	Tracey Moffatt, *A Haunting* 2021–2023
p. 48	Theron Debris, *Vile Jelly* 2023
p. 49	Theron Debris, *Fortuna* 2023
p. 50	Theron Debris, *Chuparrosa* 2023
p. 51	Theron Debris, *Amniotic* 2023
p. 52-53	Minyoung Kim, *The Bath* 2021
p. 54-55	Minyoung Kim, *The Knife*, 2021
p. 56-57	Clare Milledge, *Badb: bro im glitched* 2023. Photo: Jessica Maurer.
p. 58-59	Marianna Simnett, *The Udder* 2014 (still)
p. 60-61	Marianna Simnett, *The Udder* 2014 (still)
p. 62-63	Jemima Lucas, *Stifled forces – Constantly Swelling. Will the Levee break?* 2023, installation view, PRODUCE, Melbourne. Photo: Simon Strong.
p. 64-65	Naomi Kantjuriny, *Mamu (Good Spirits)* 2023 (detail)
p. 66-67	Mia Boe, *I Suspect* 2023 (work in progress)
p. 68-69	Kellie Wells, studio portrait of work in progress. Photo: Tim Neal
p. 70-71	Zamara Zamara, *Like Pulling Teeth* 2023
p. 72-73	Suzan Pitt, *Visitation* 2011 (stills)
p. 74-75	Julia Robinson, *Burrow Mump* 2022 (detail)
p. 76	Julia Robinson, *Tatterdemalion* 2022 (installation view)

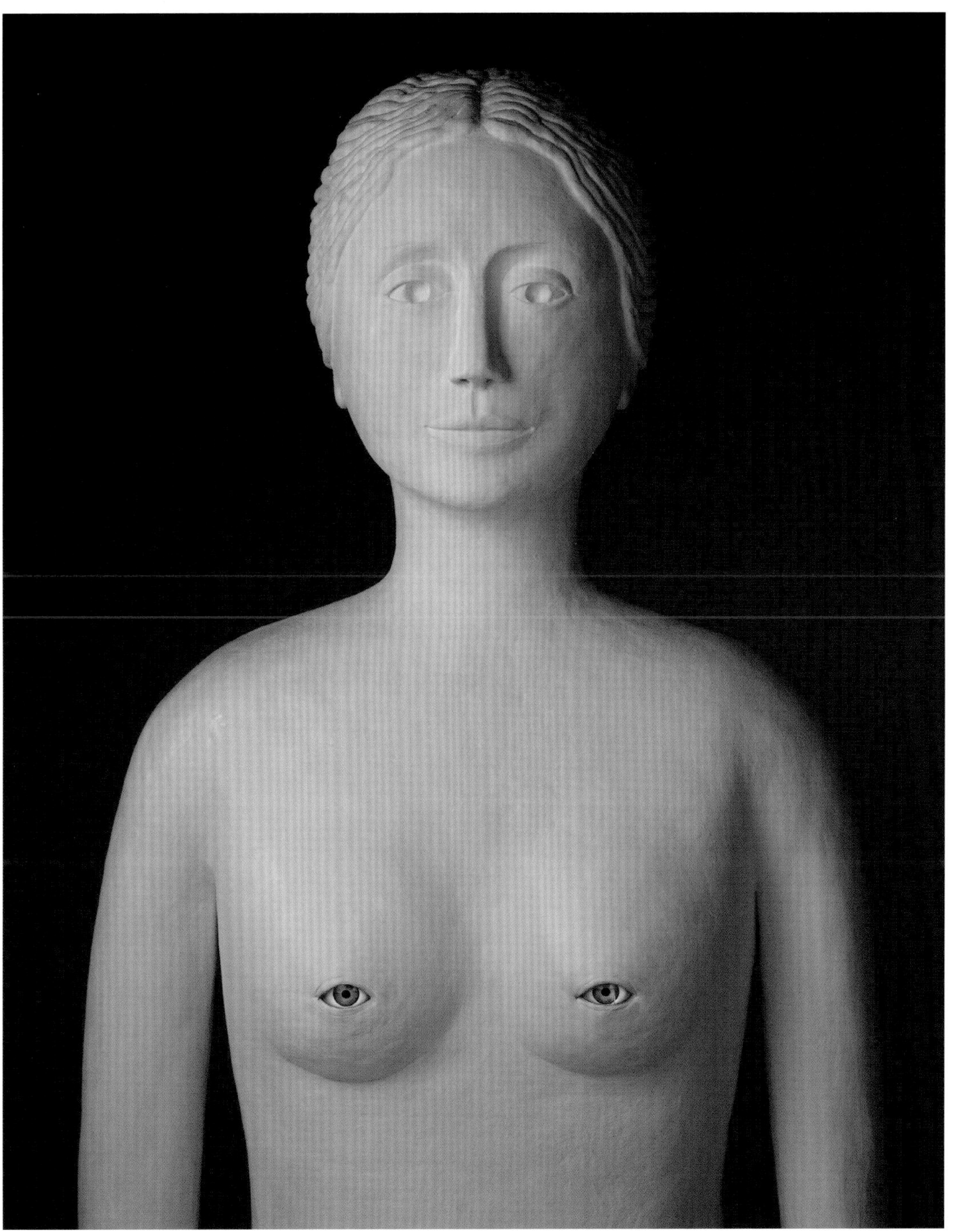

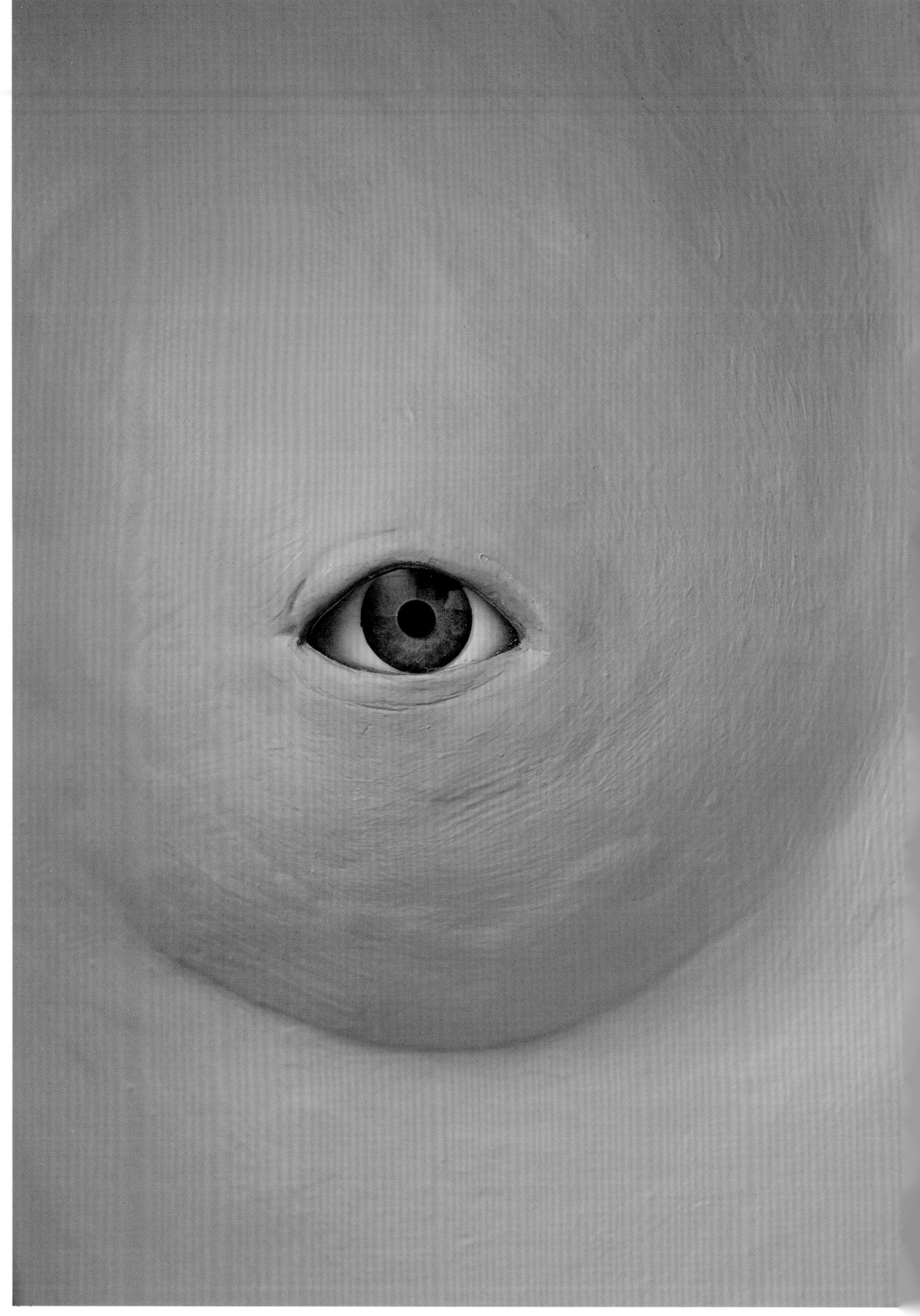

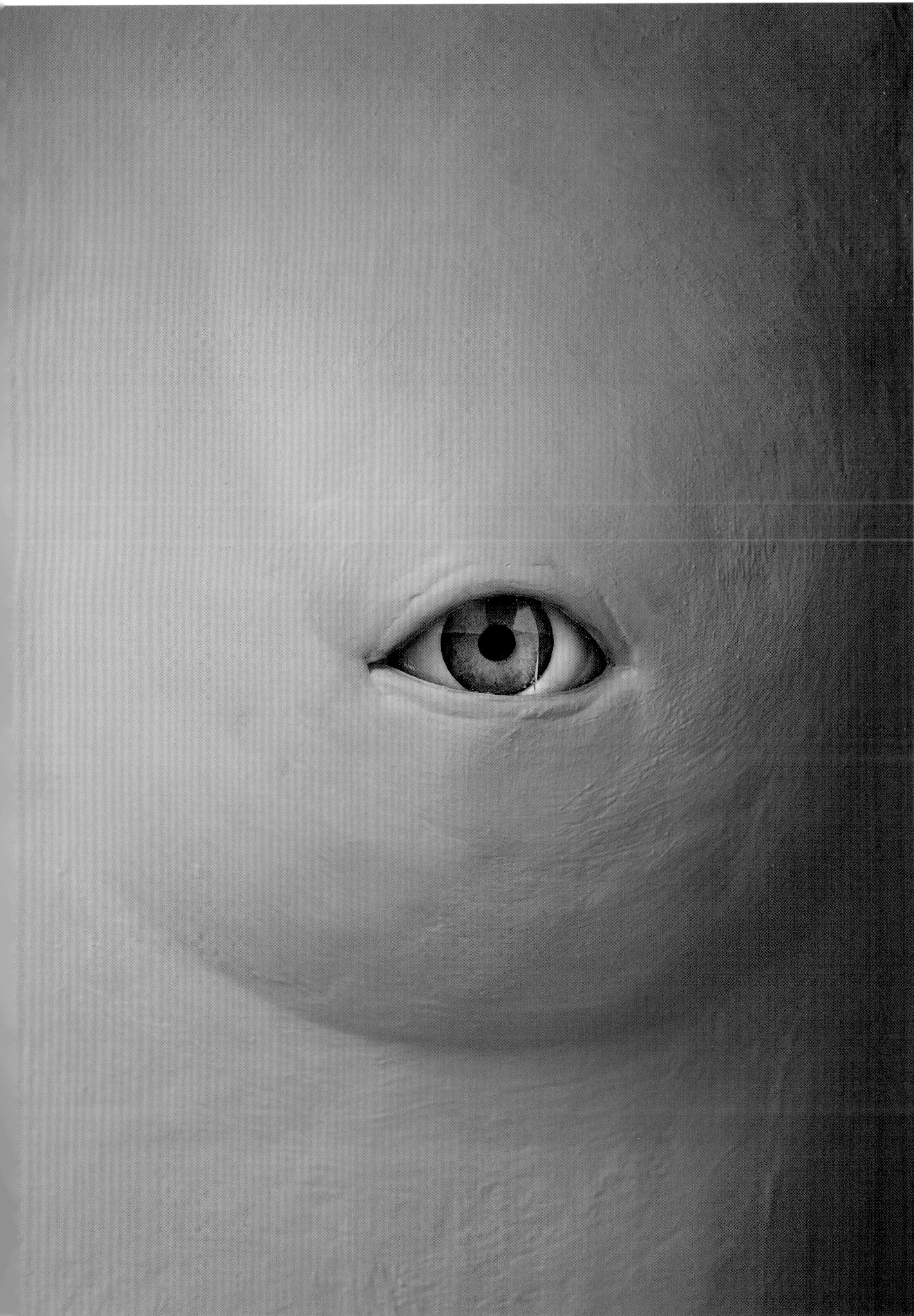

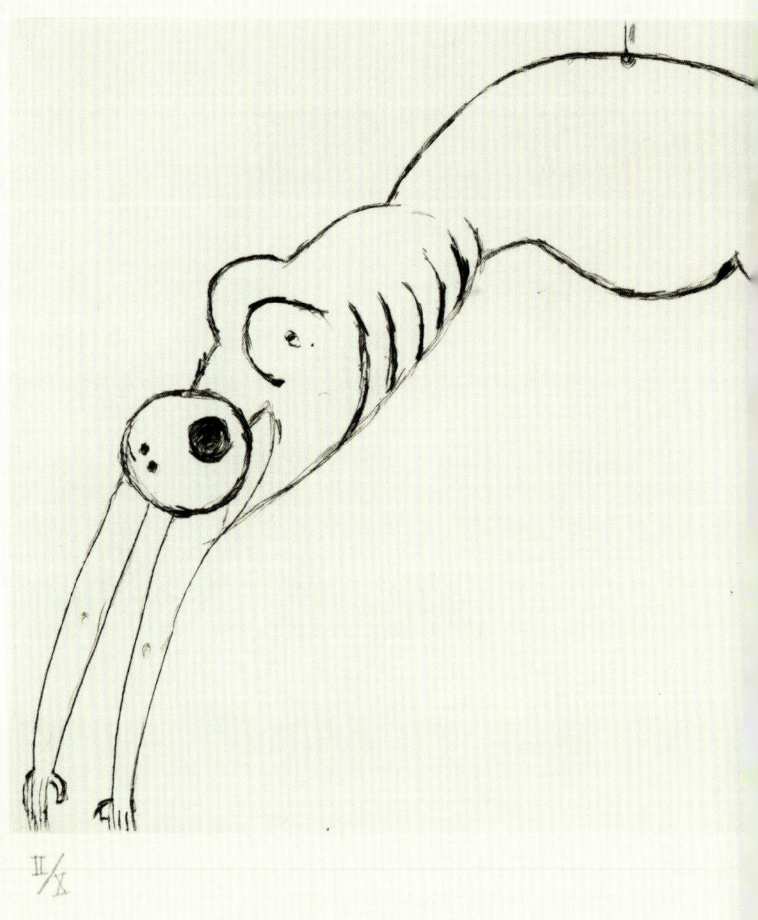

II/X

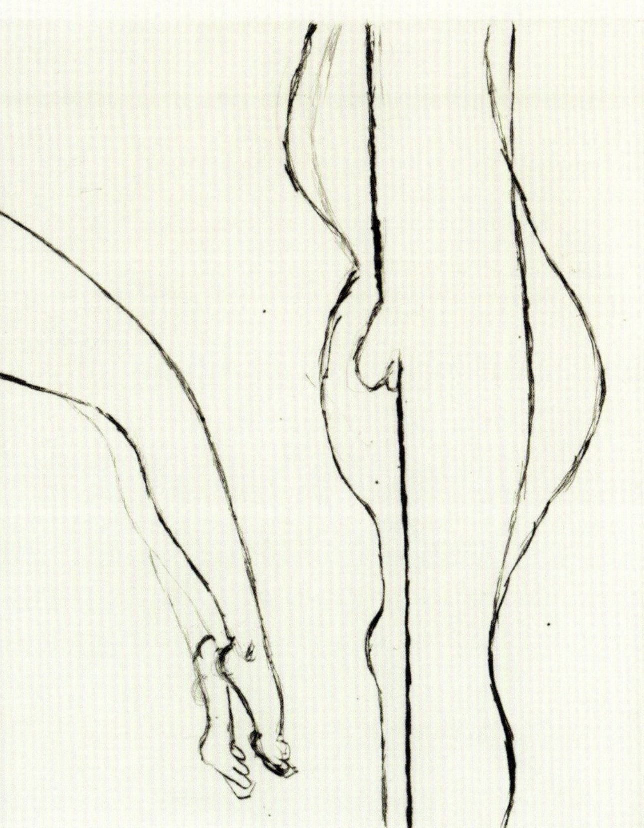
Louise Bourgeois.

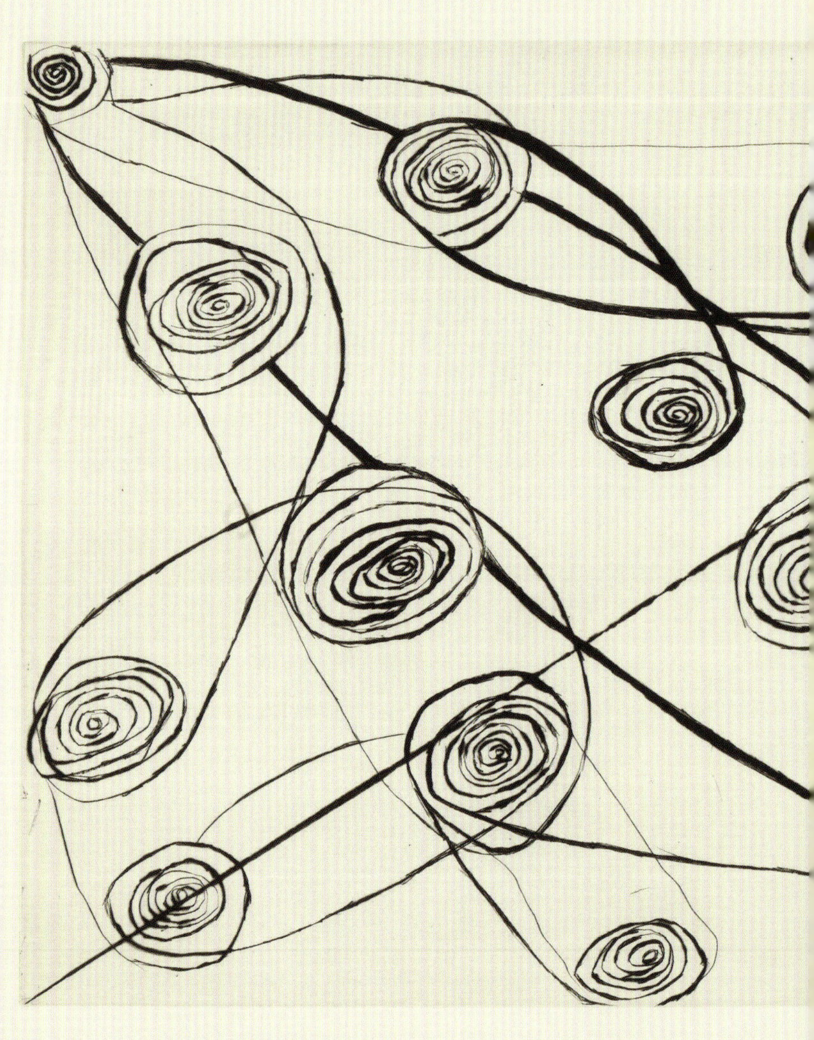

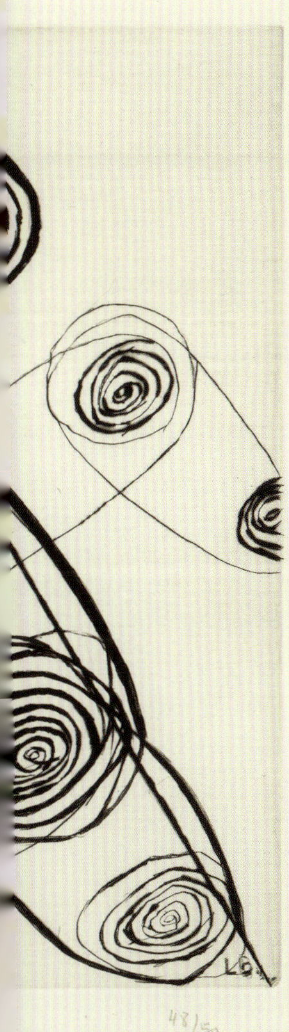
LB
48/50
Louise Bourgeois

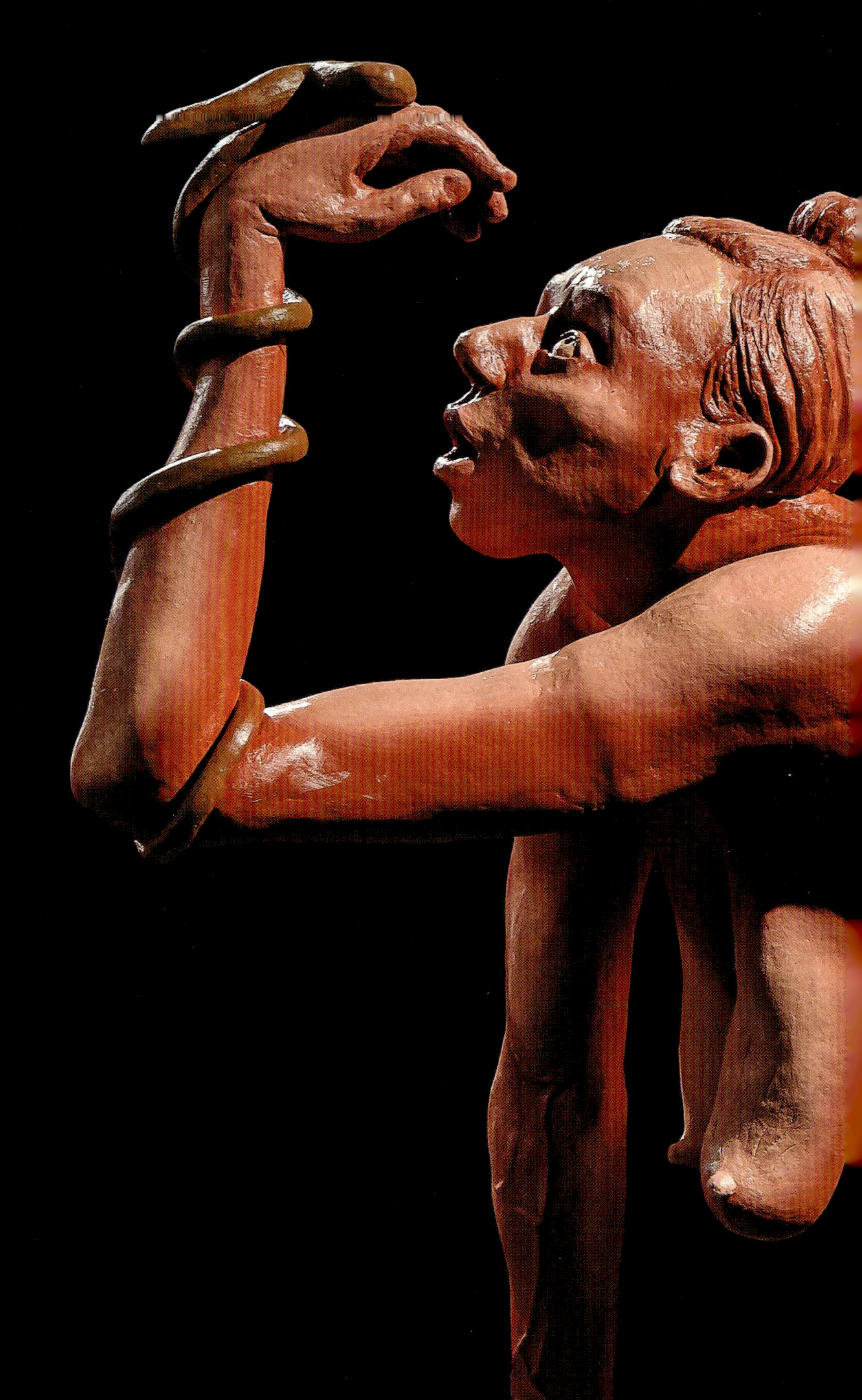

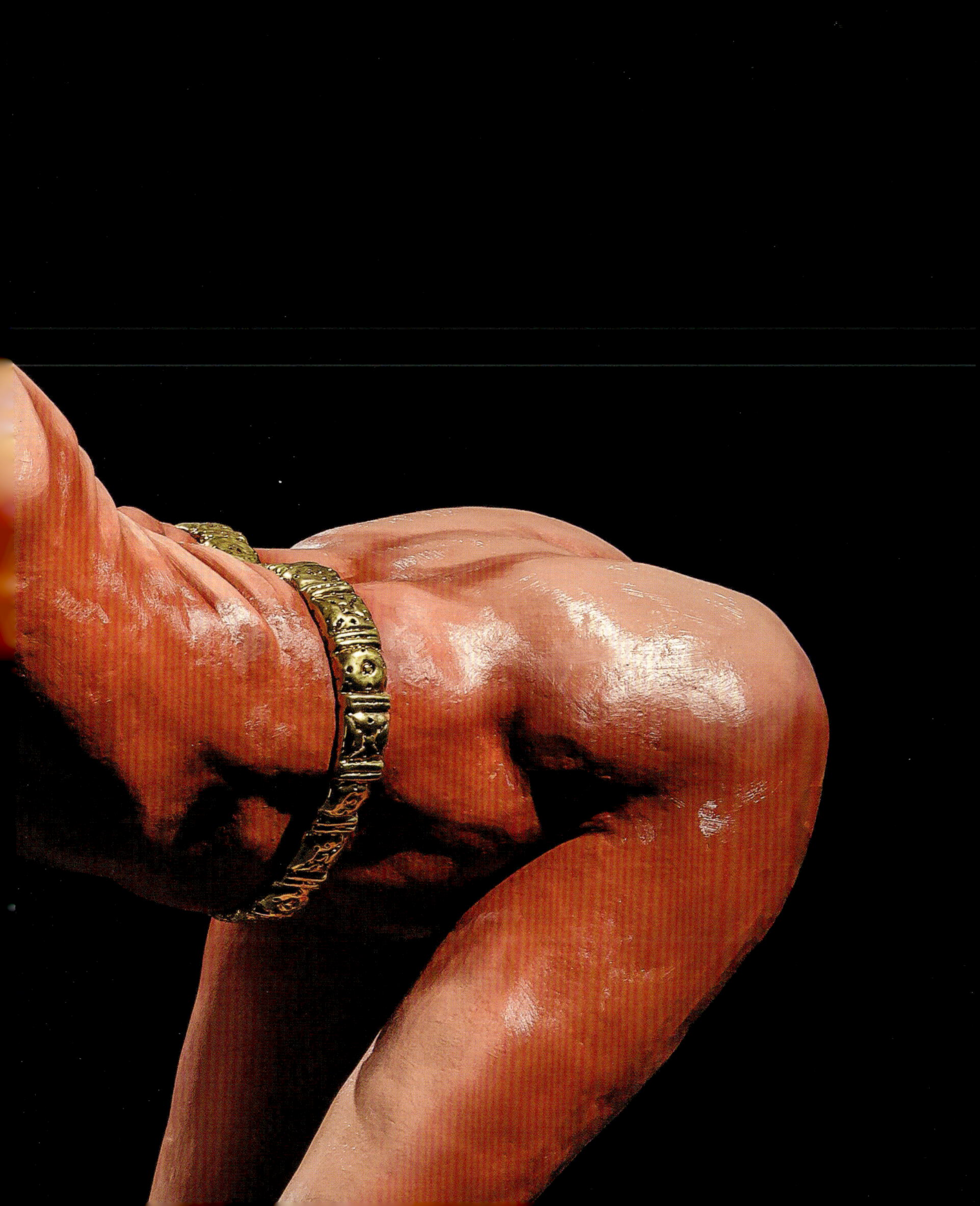

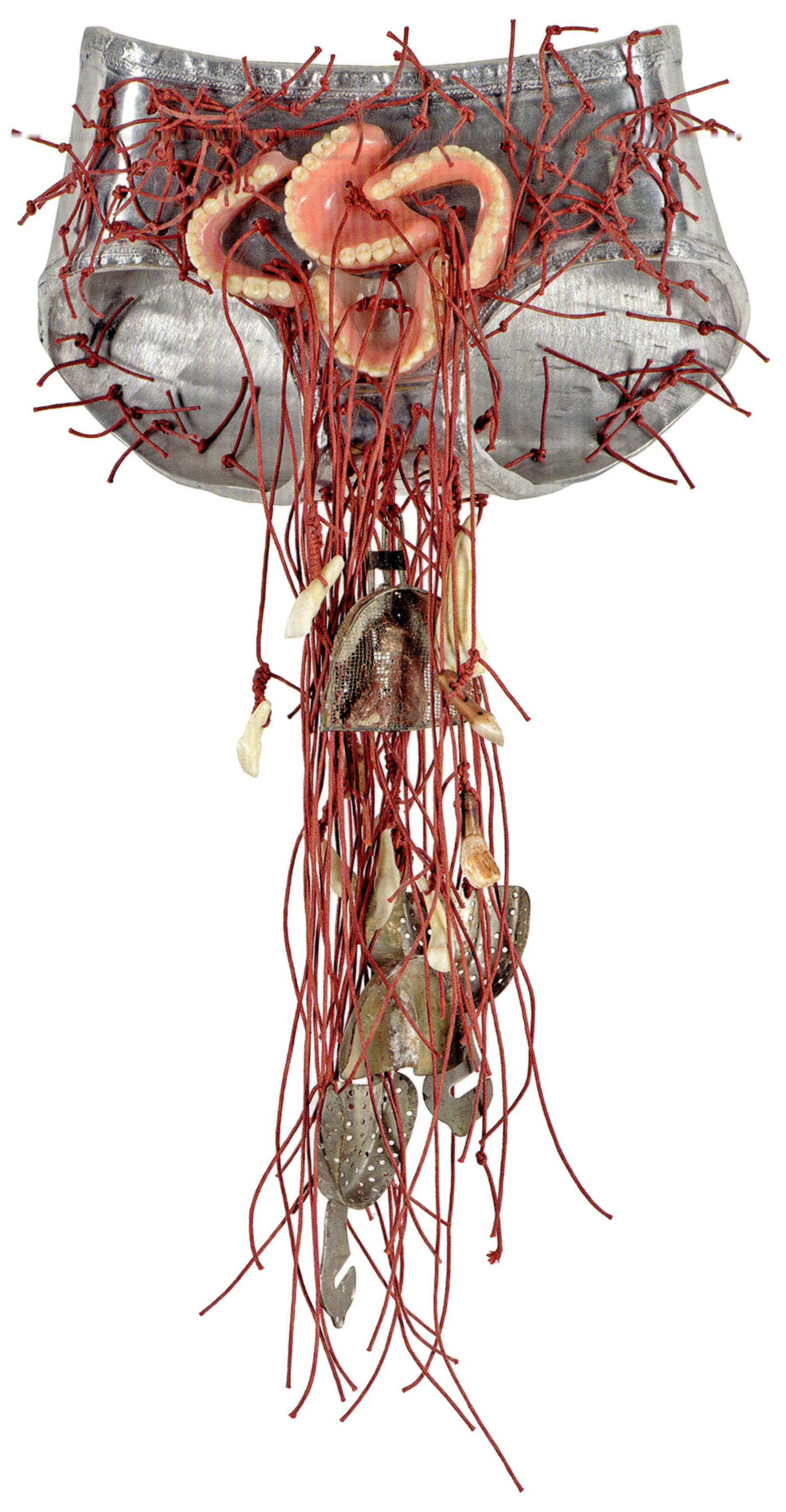

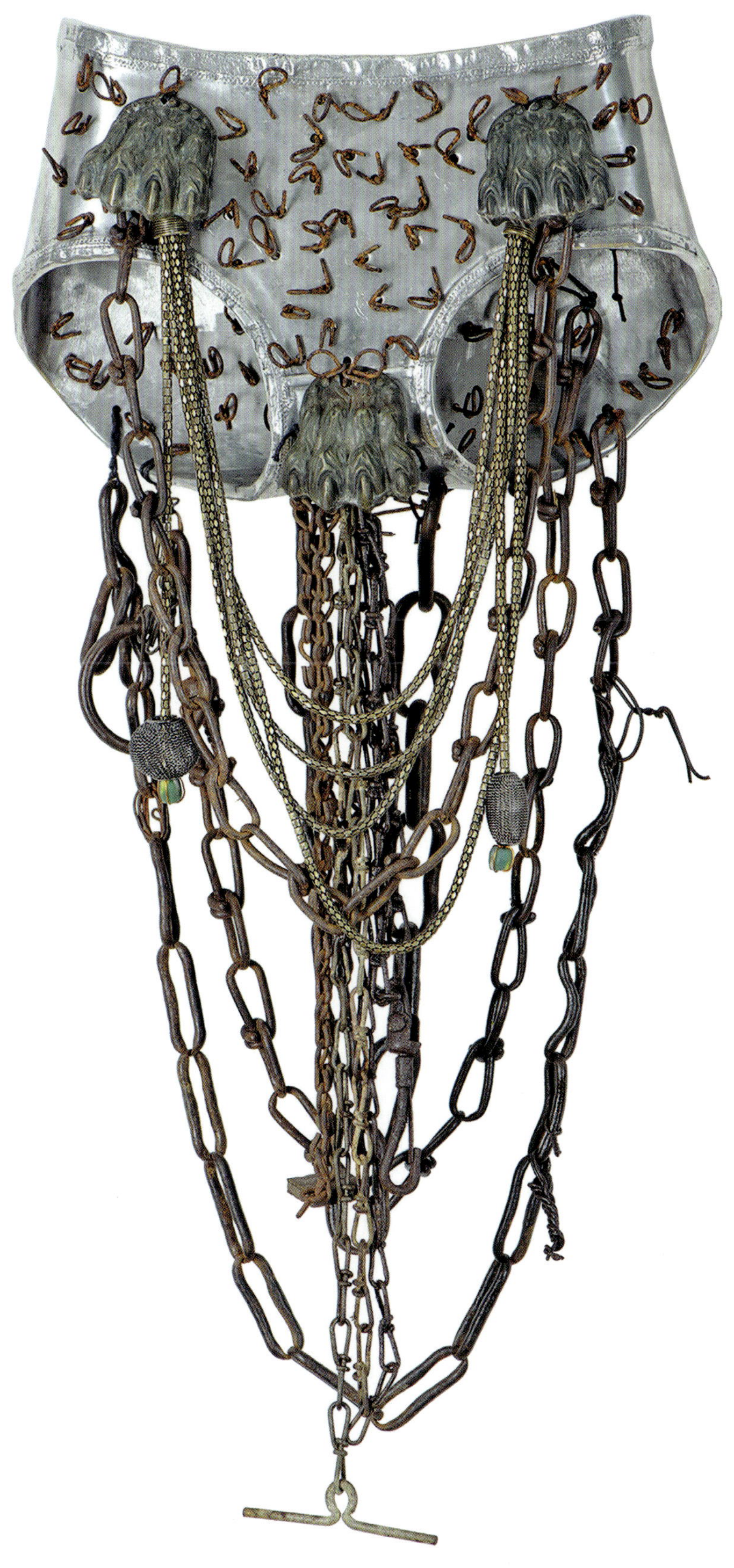

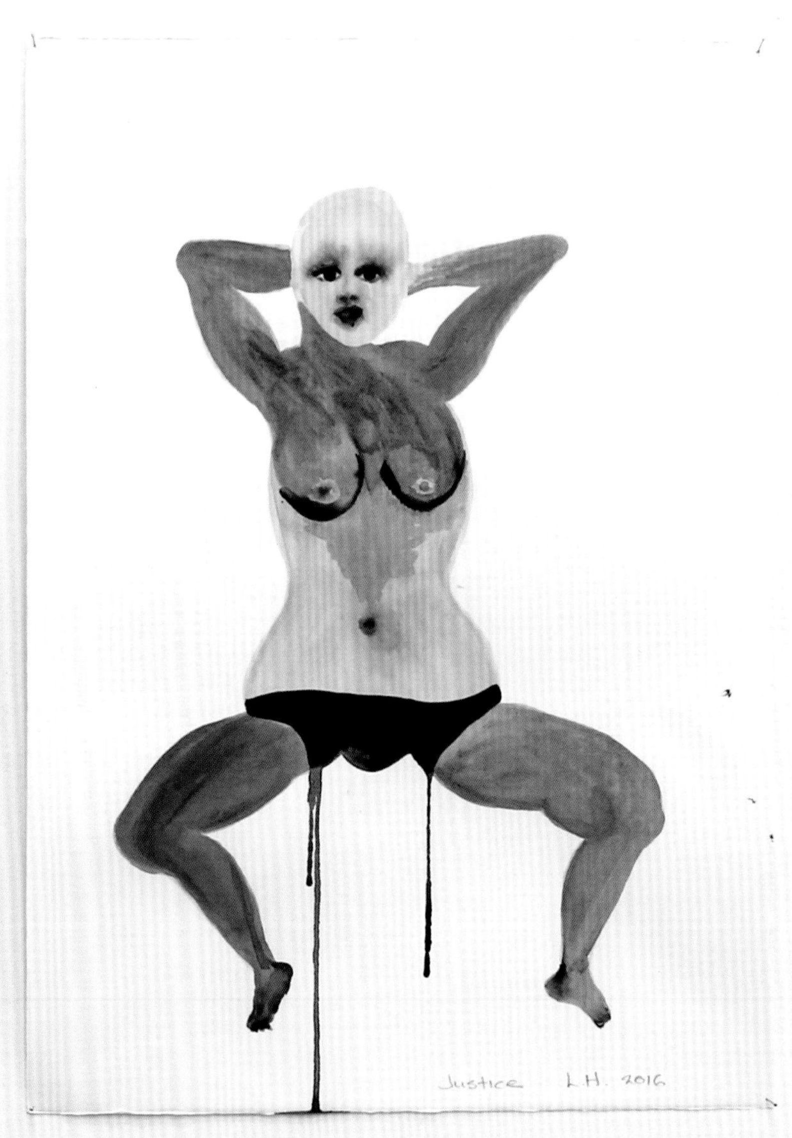
Justice L.H. 2016

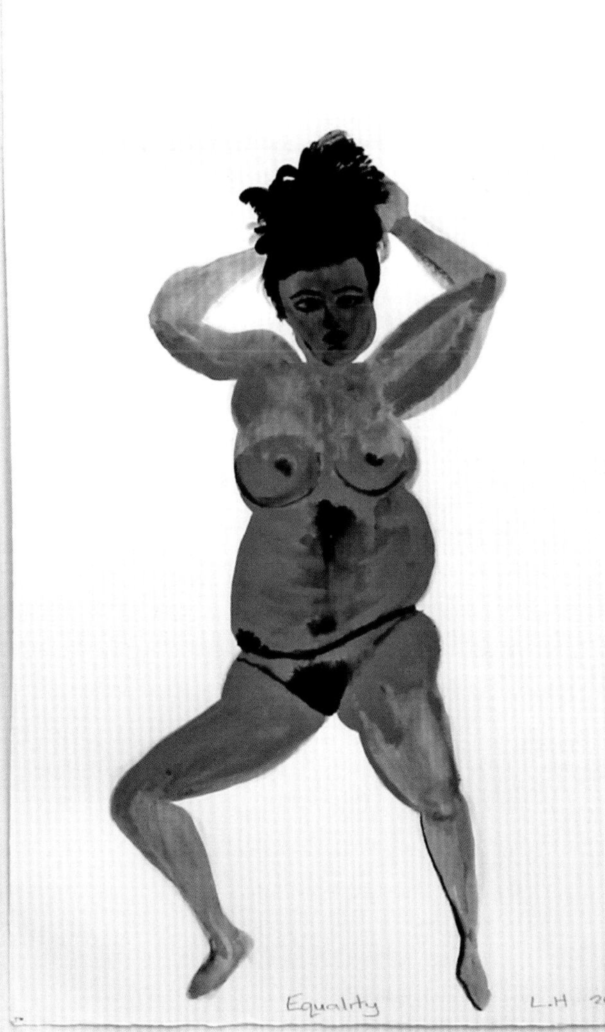
Equality
L.H 2016

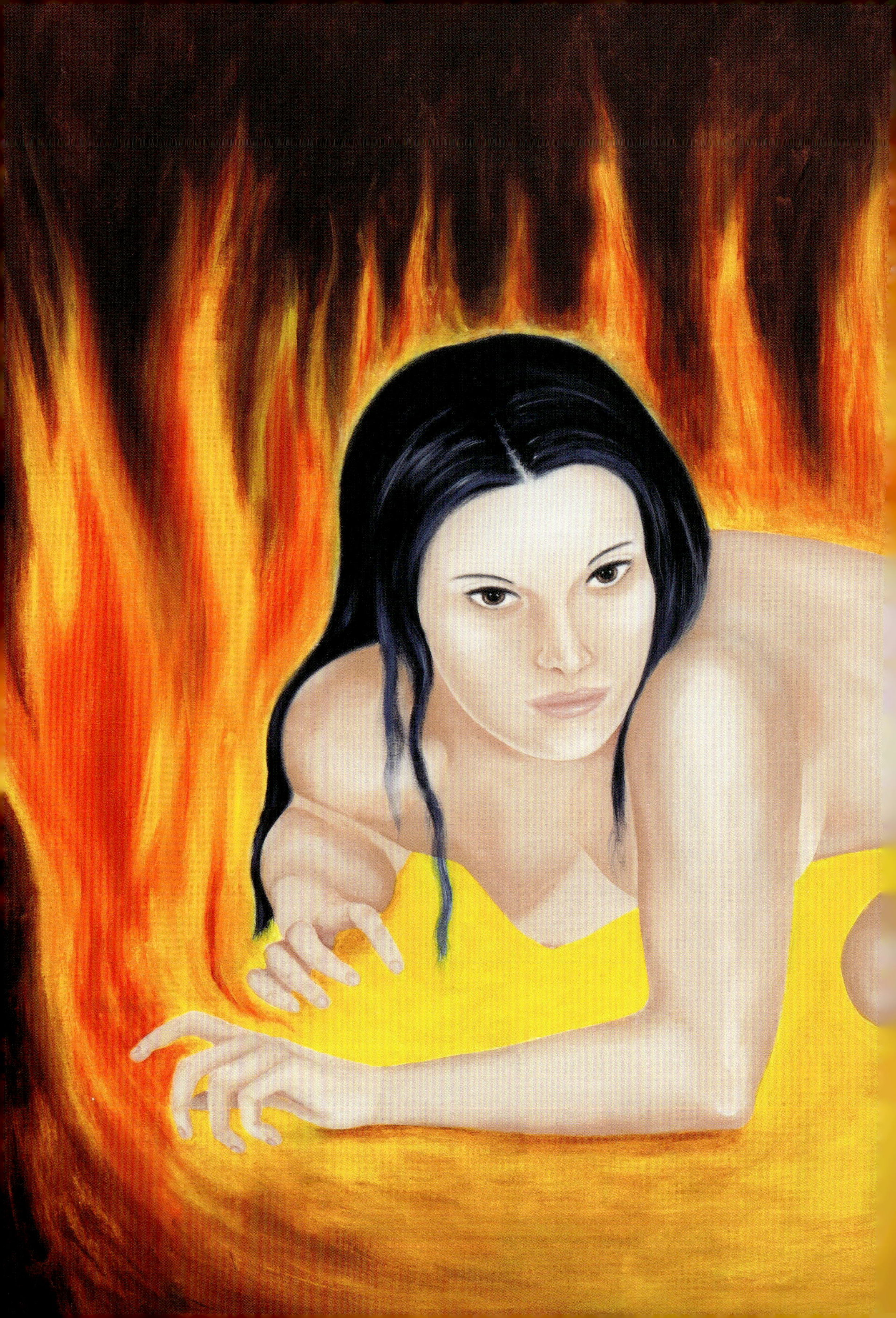

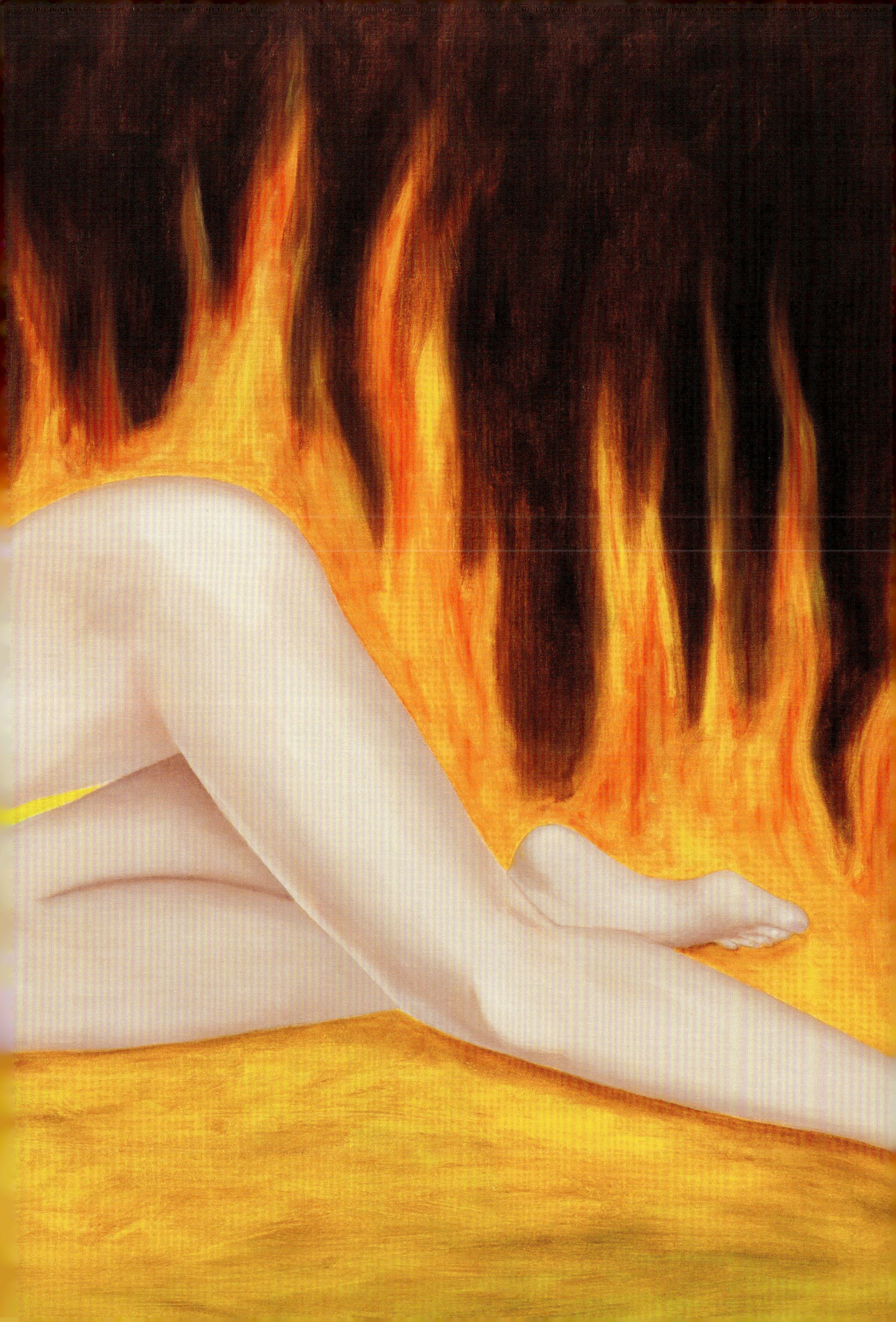

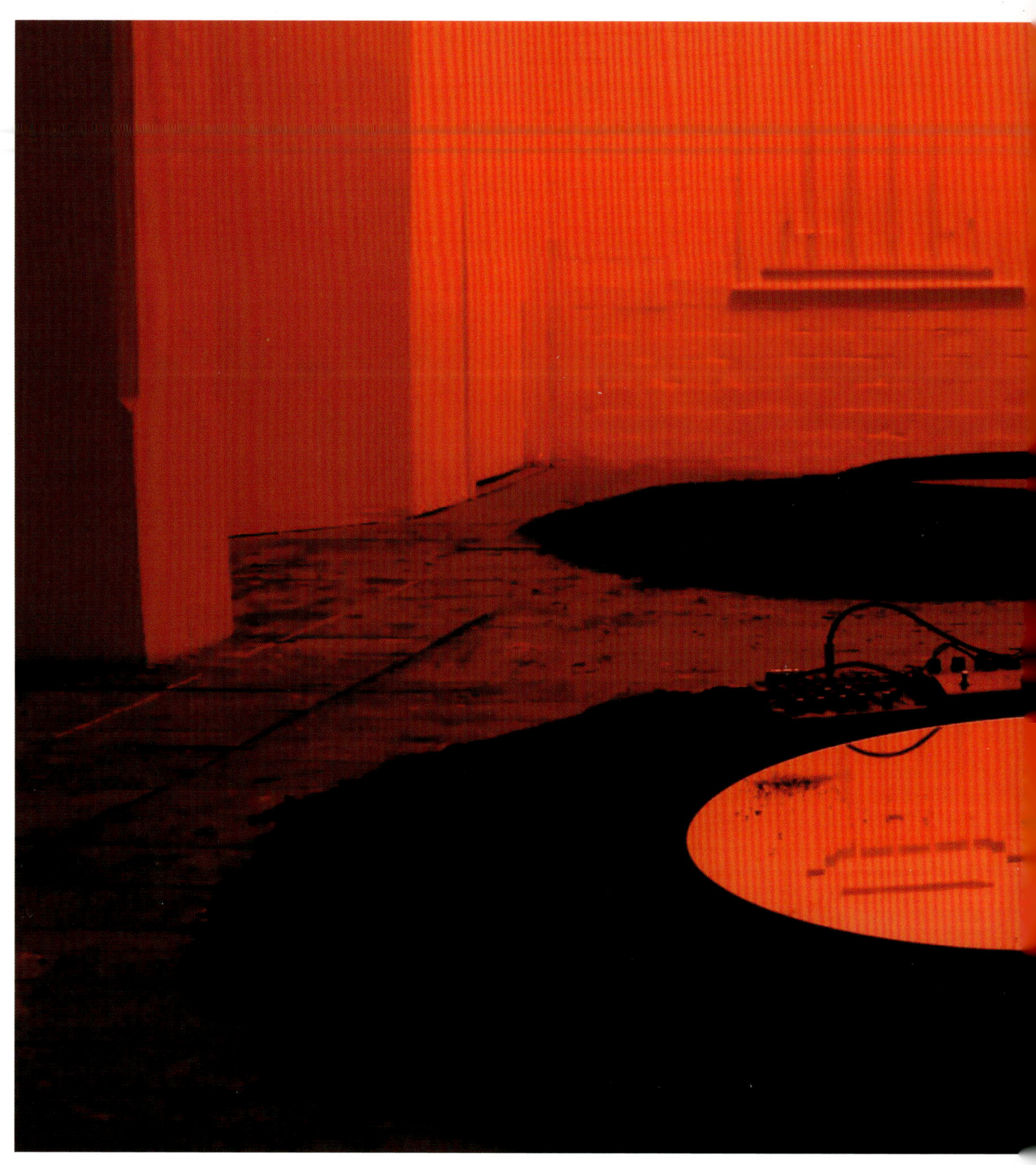

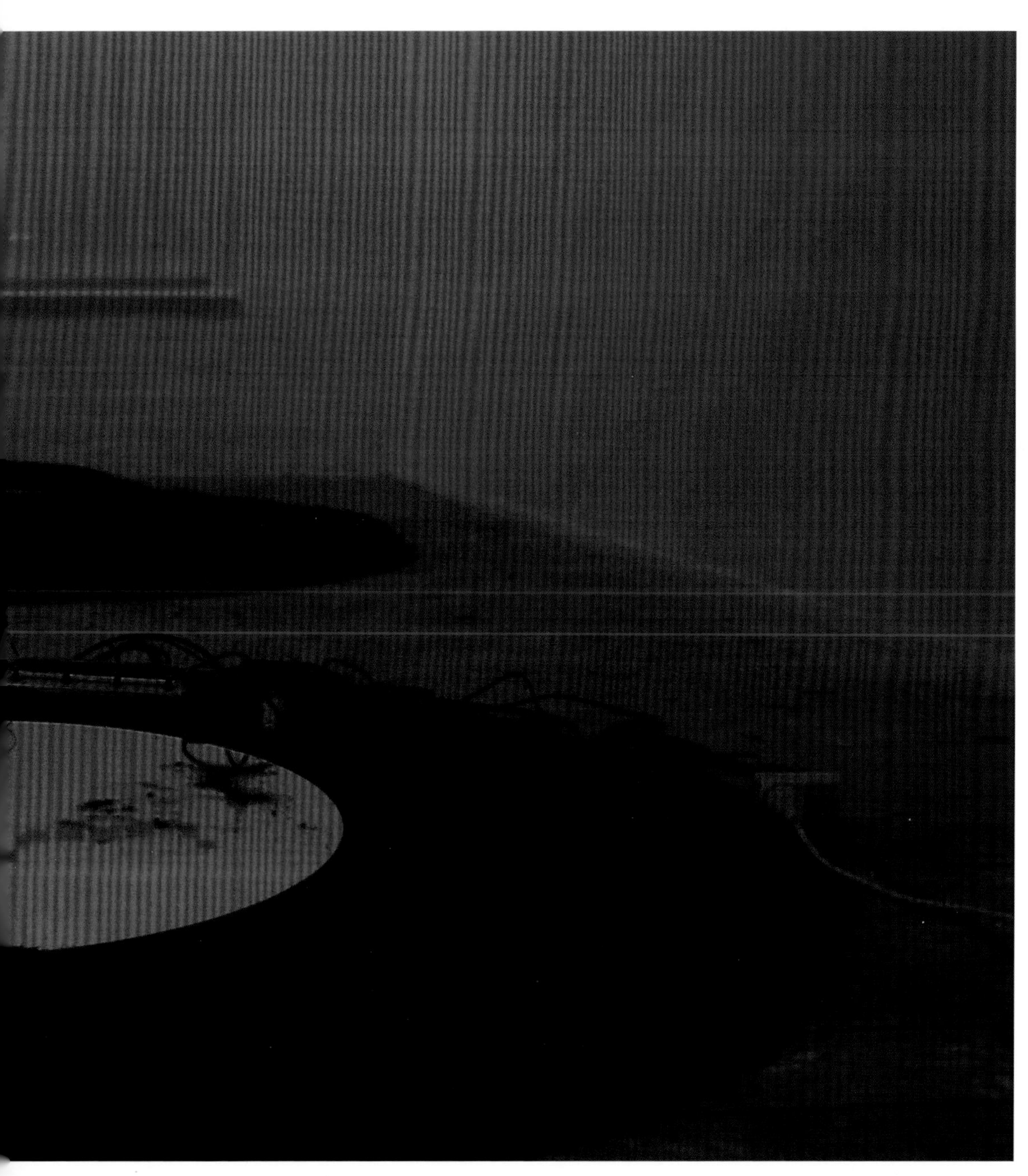

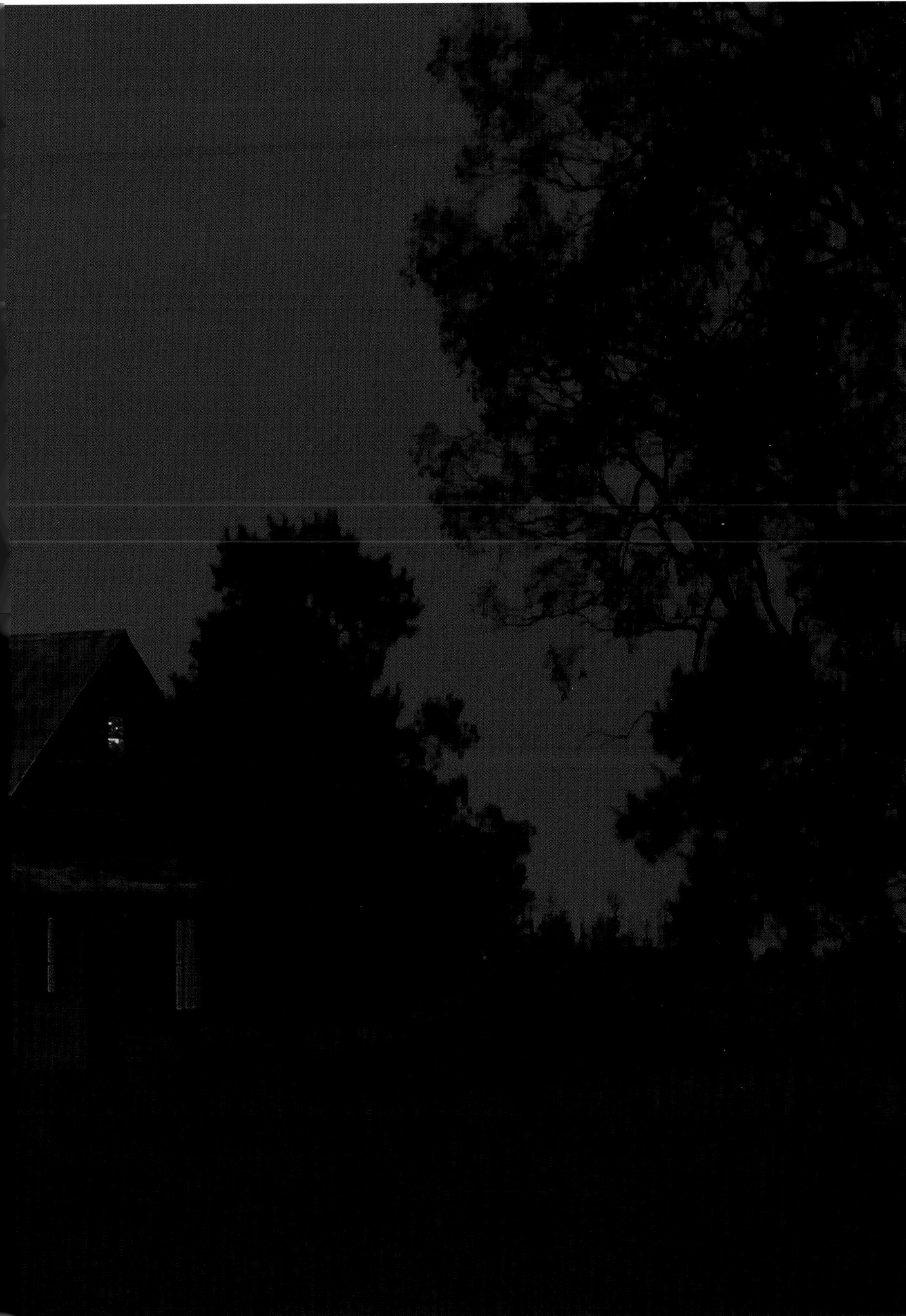

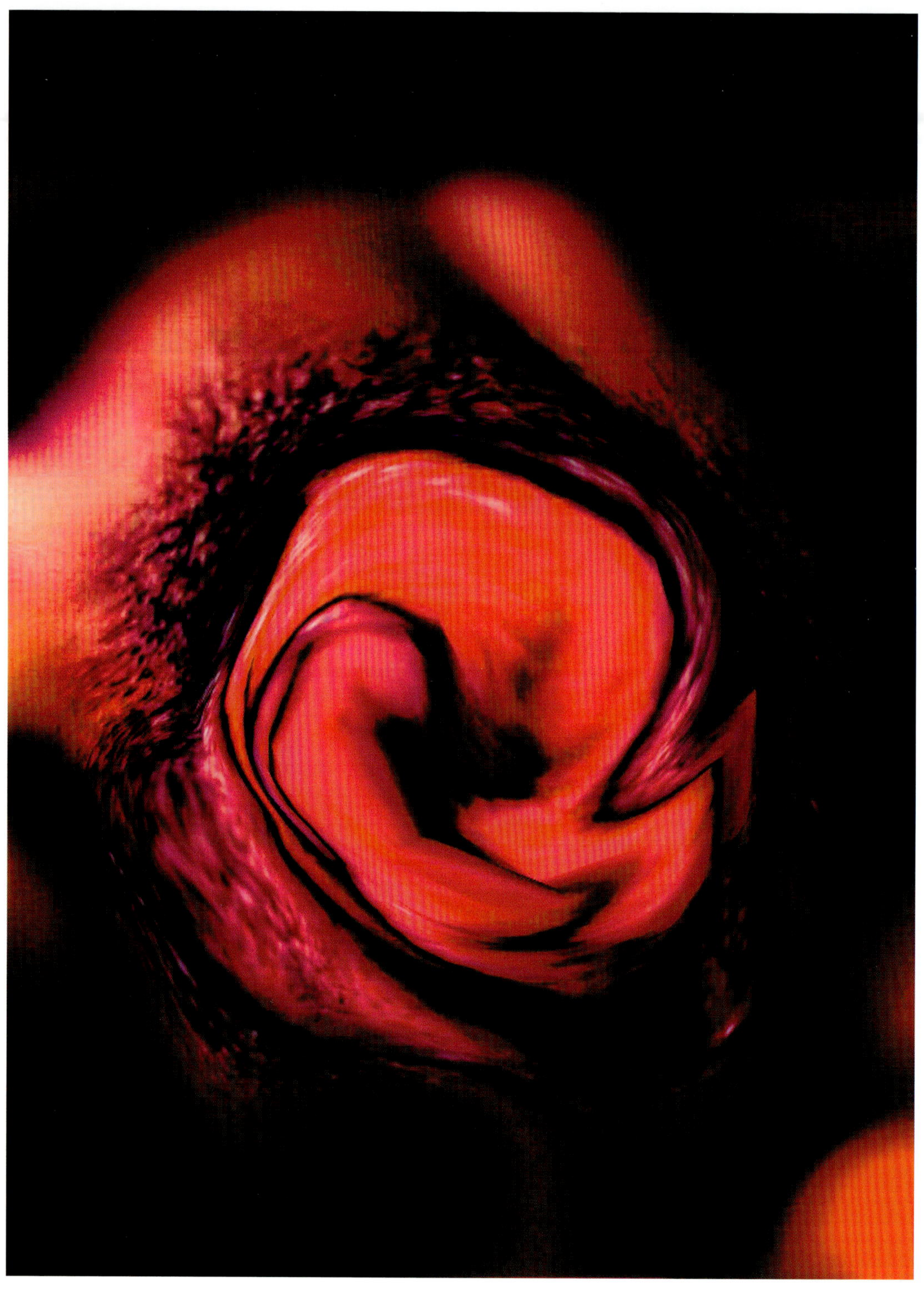

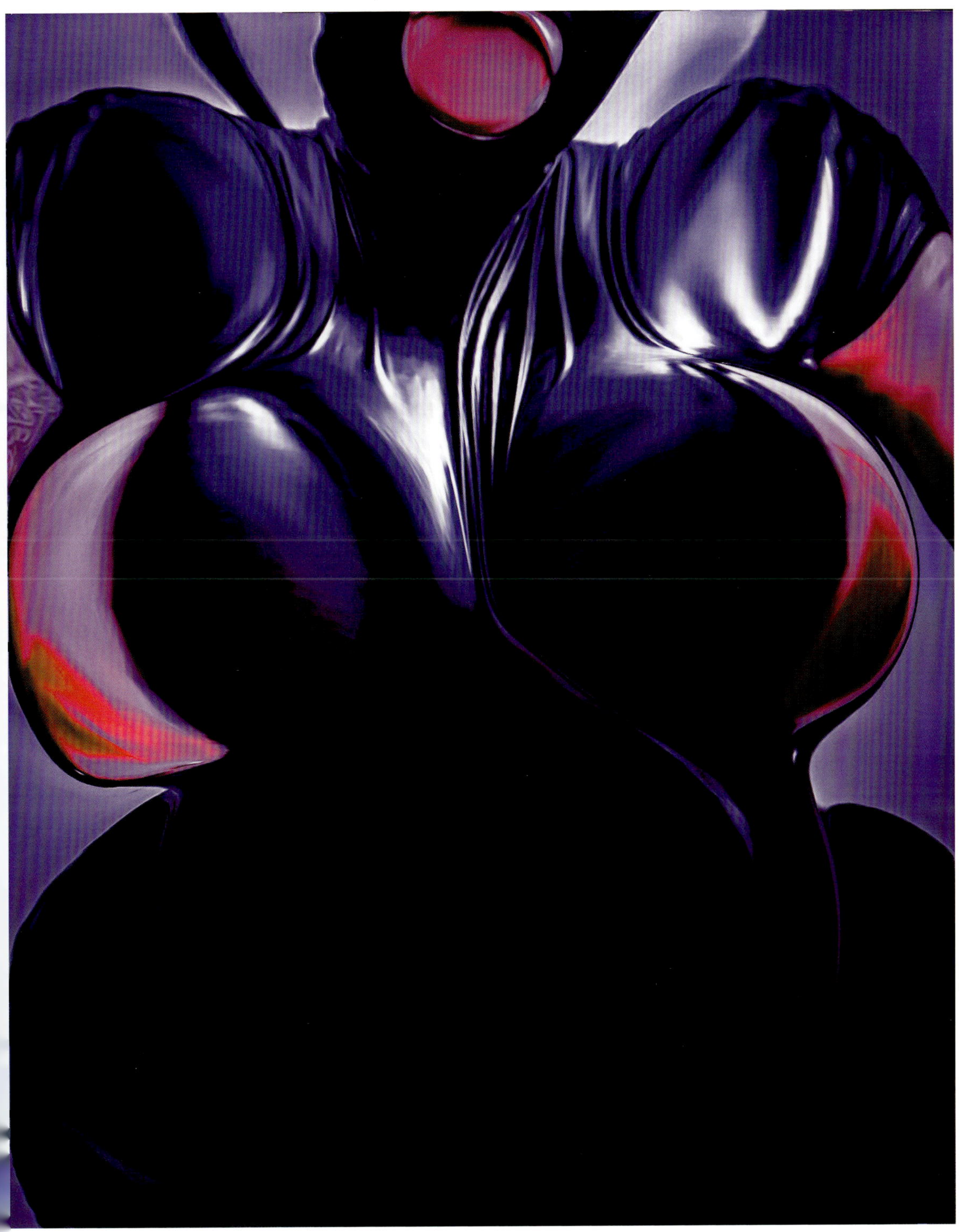

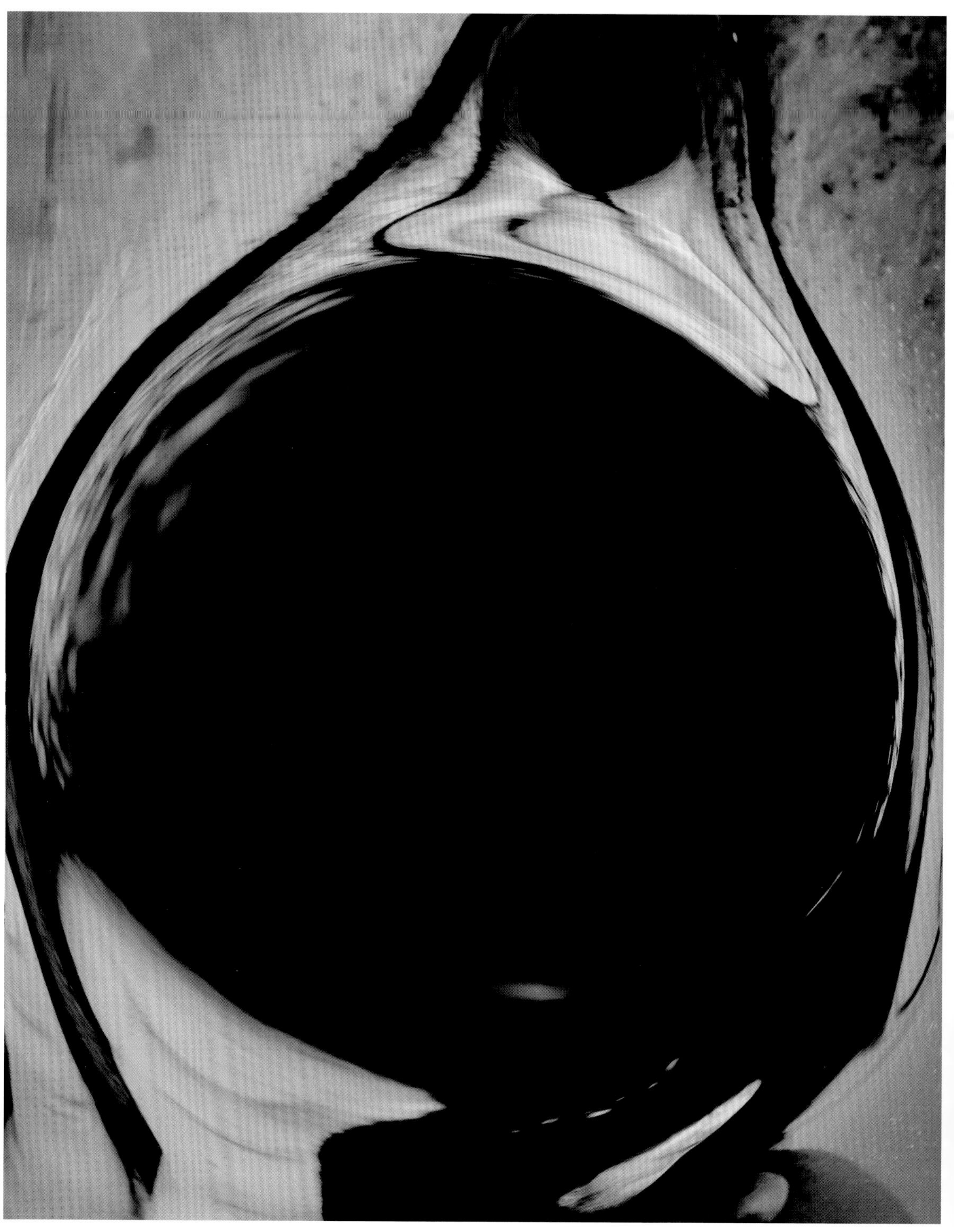

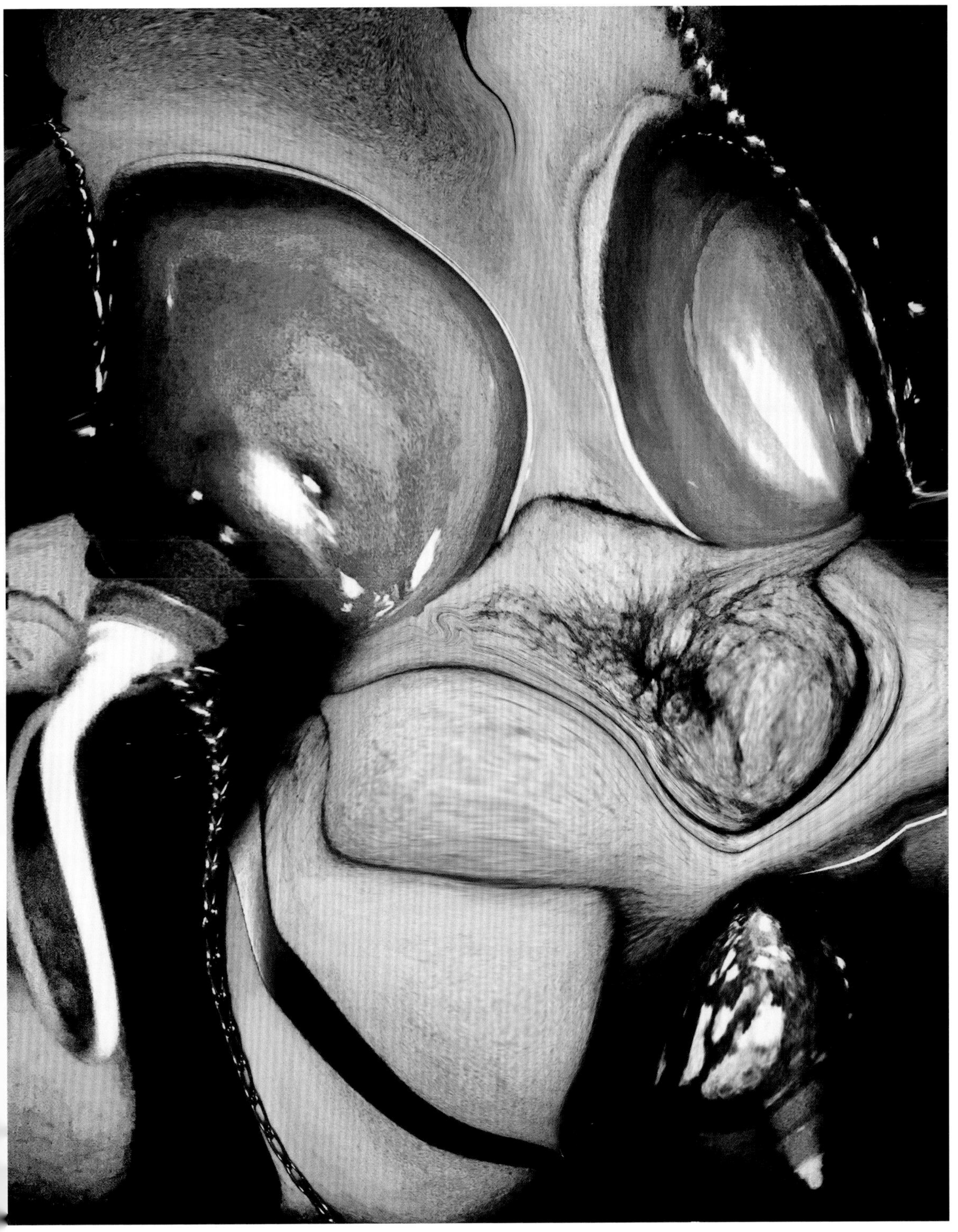

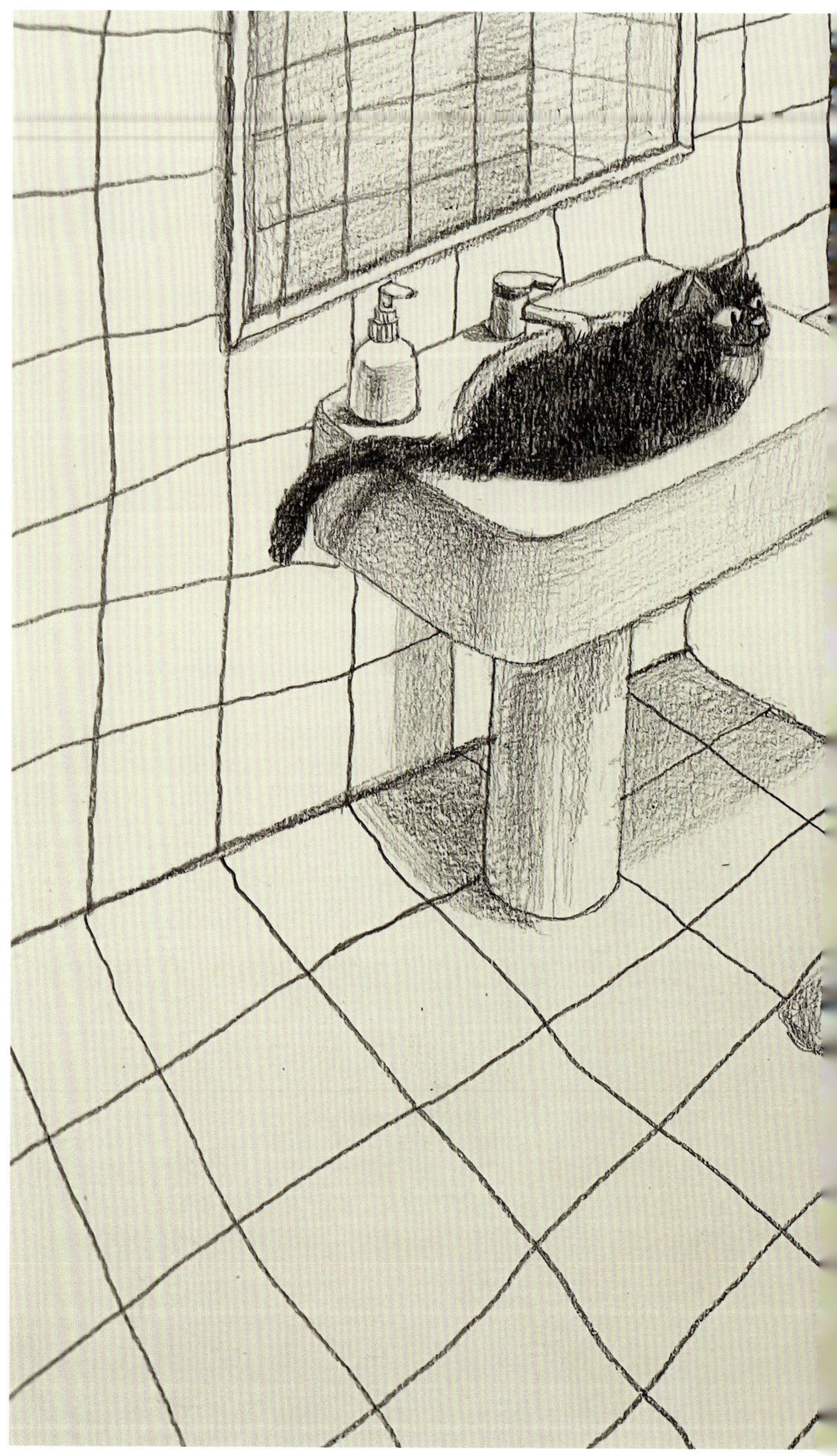

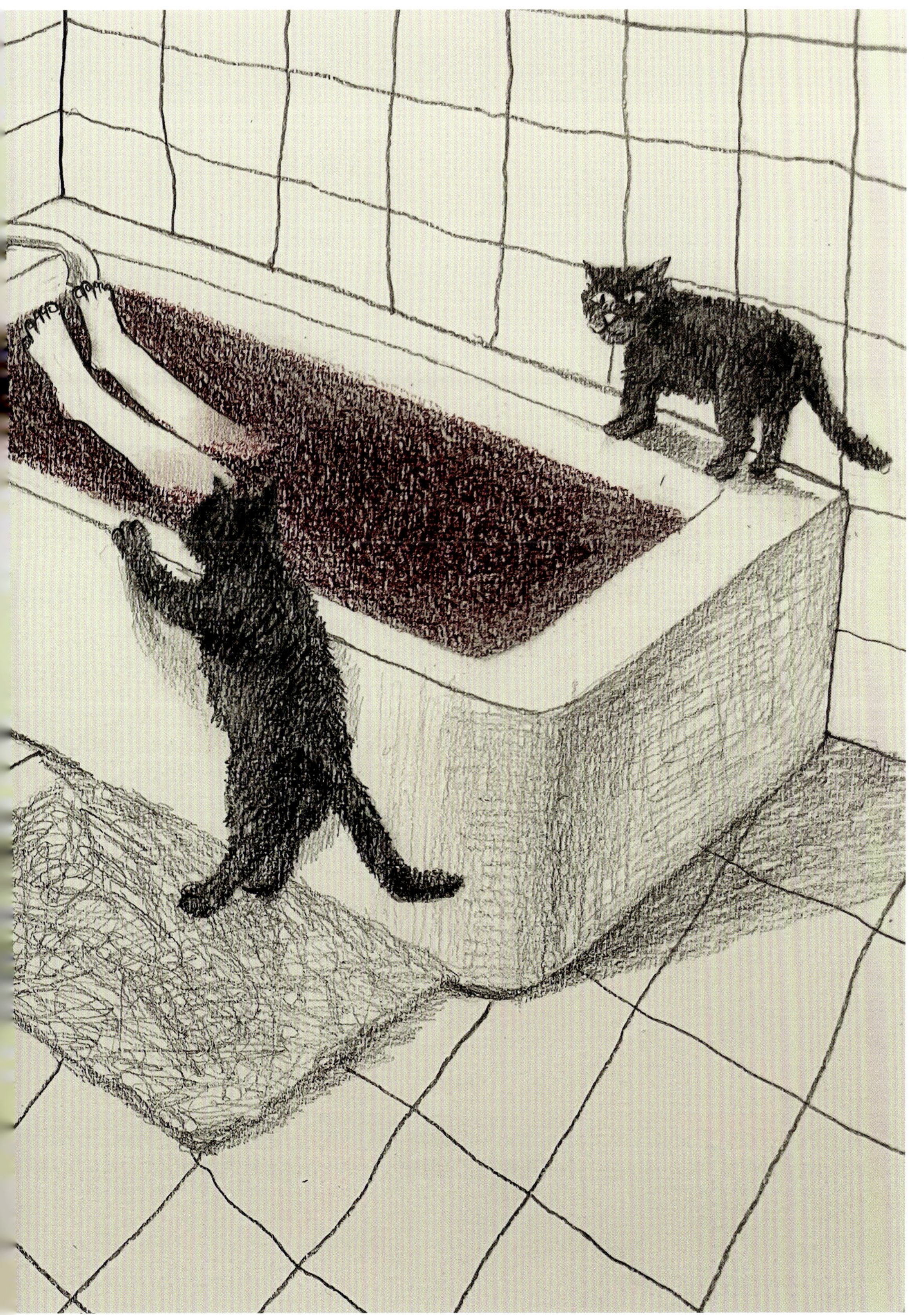

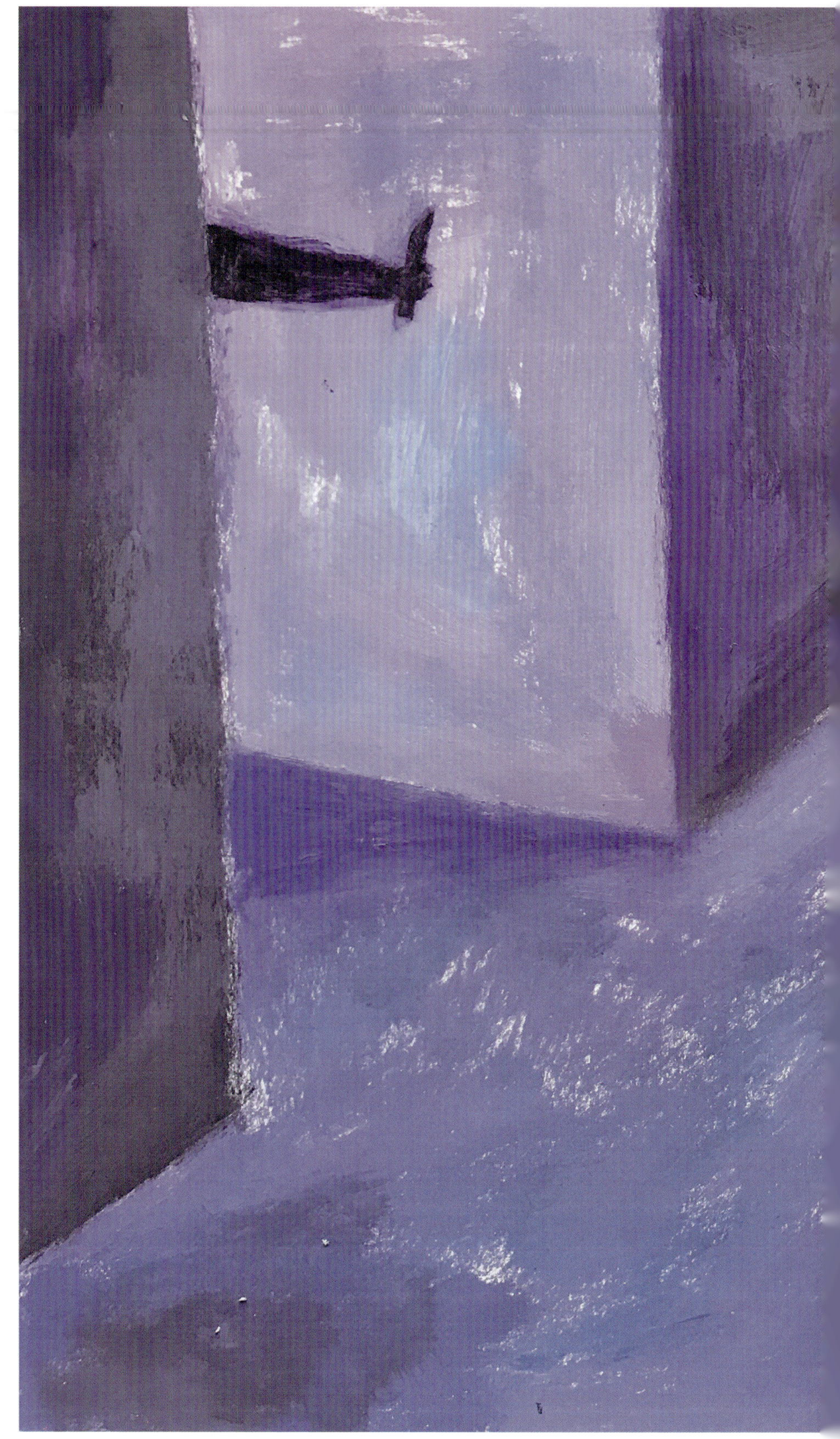

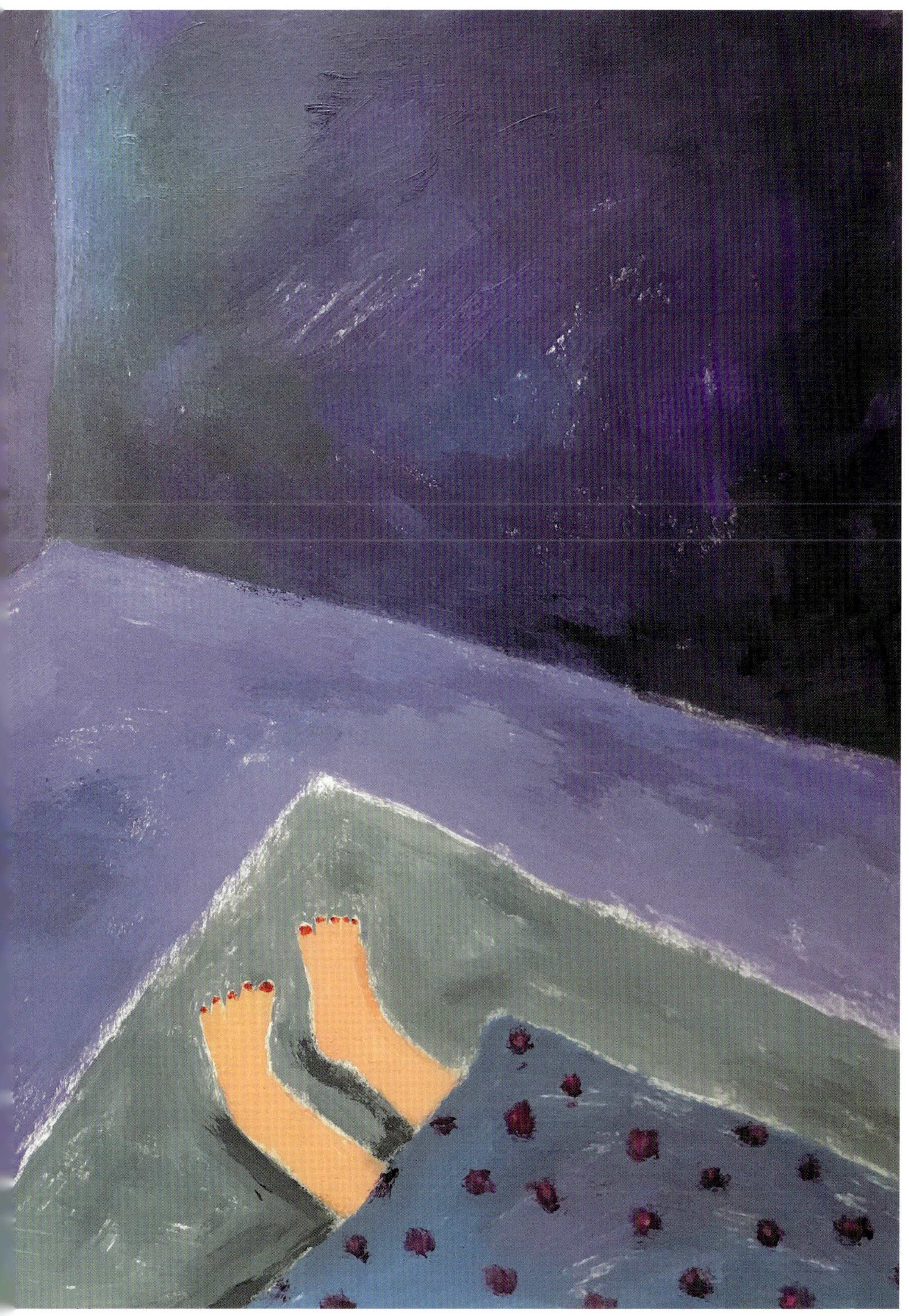

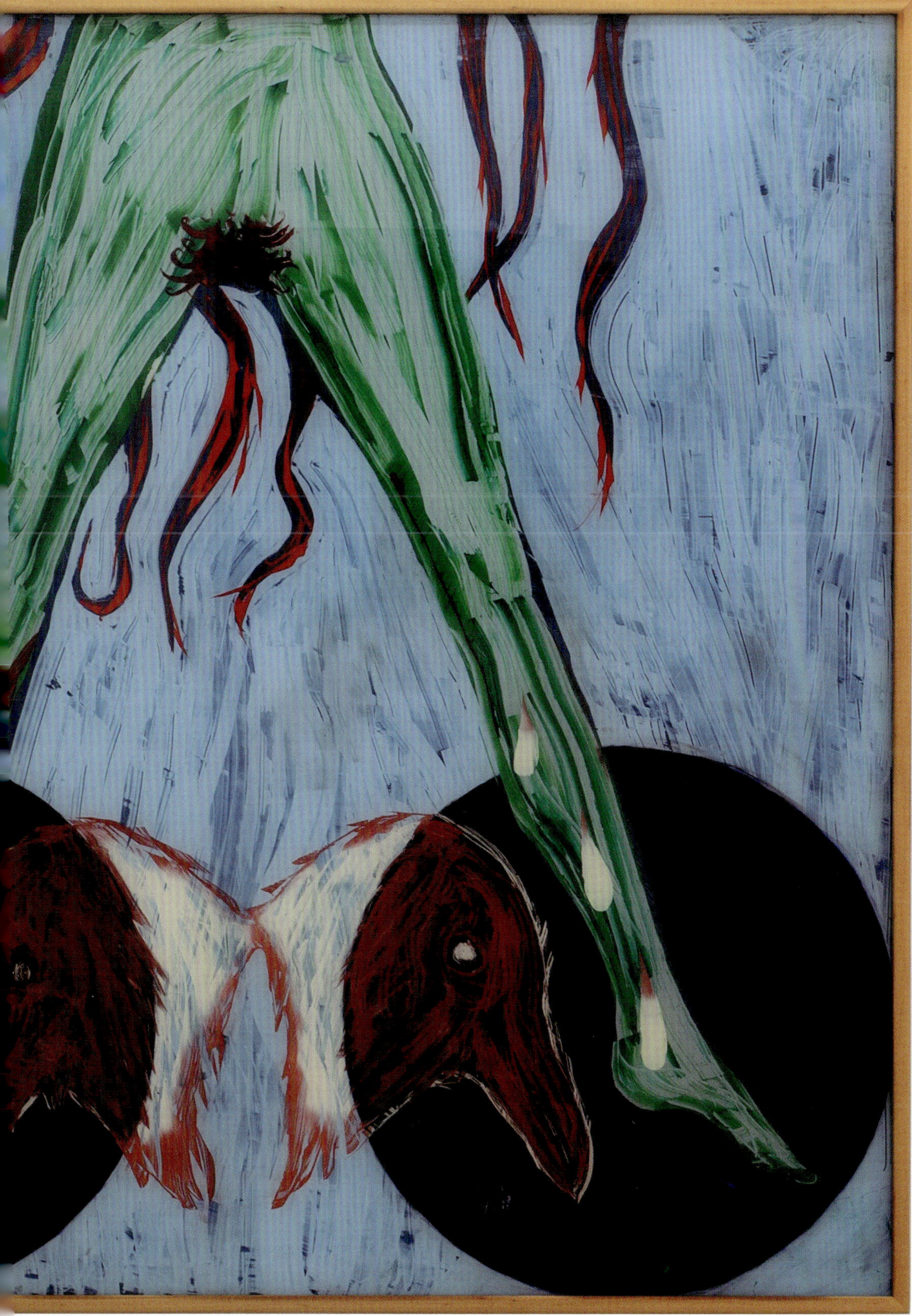

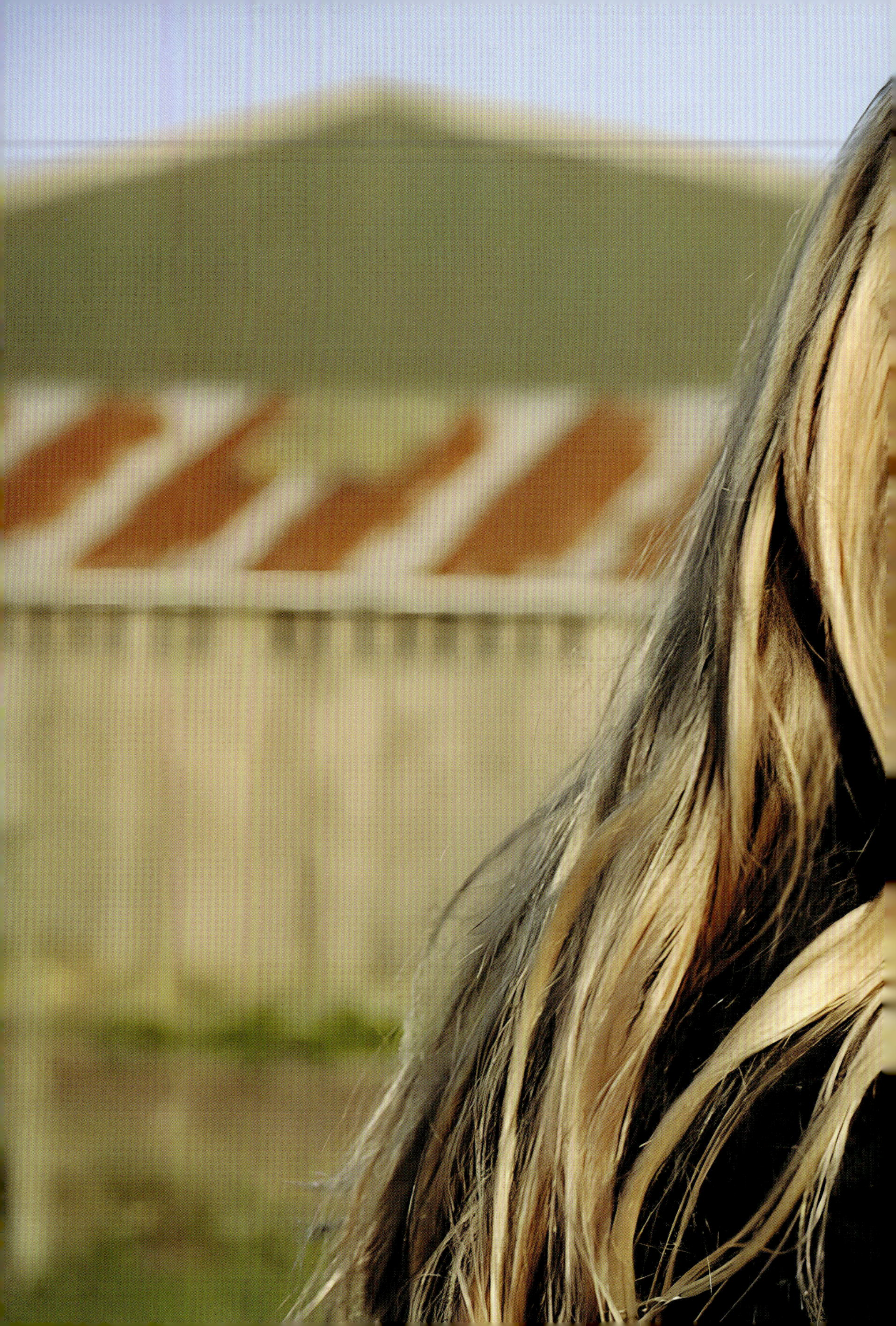

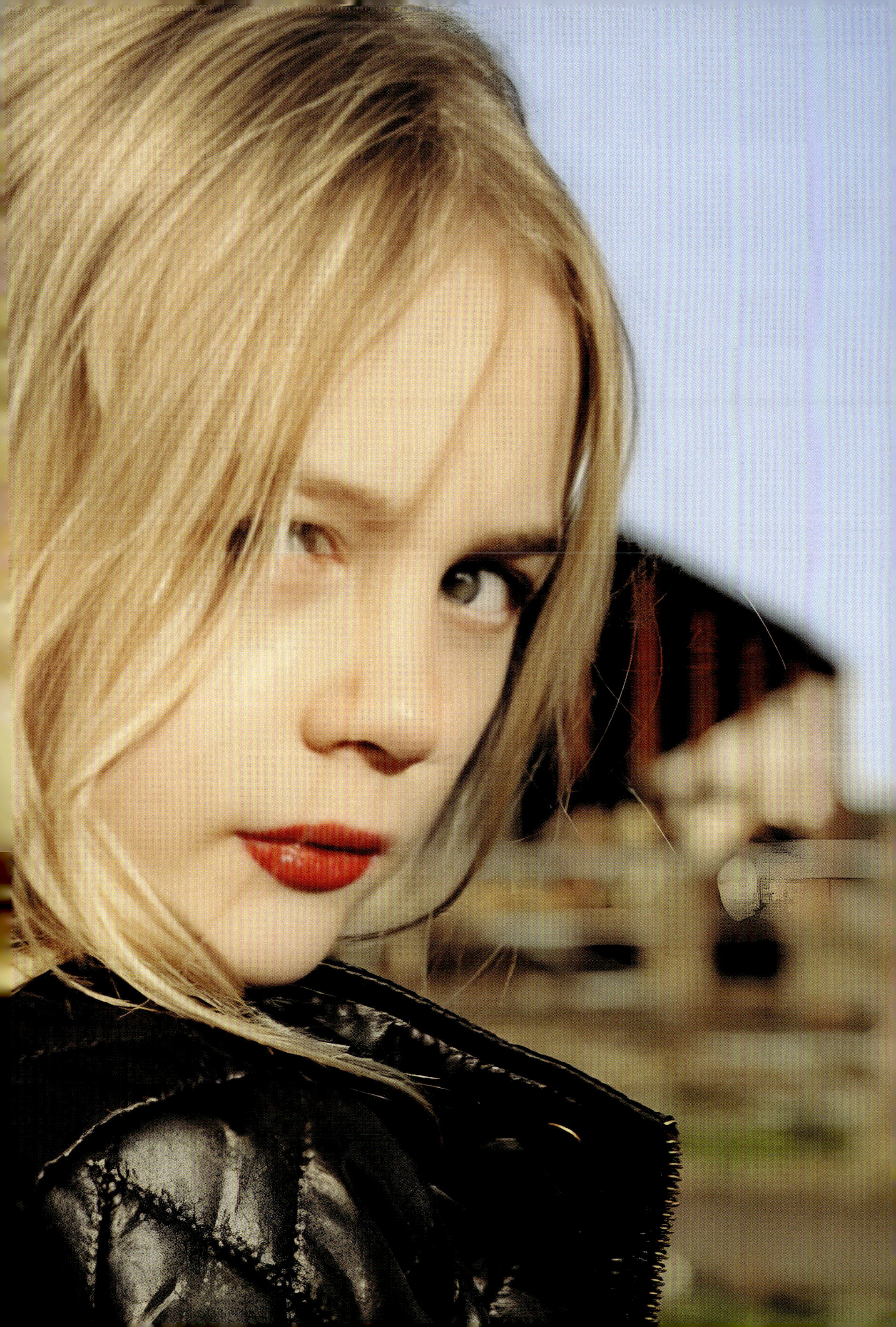

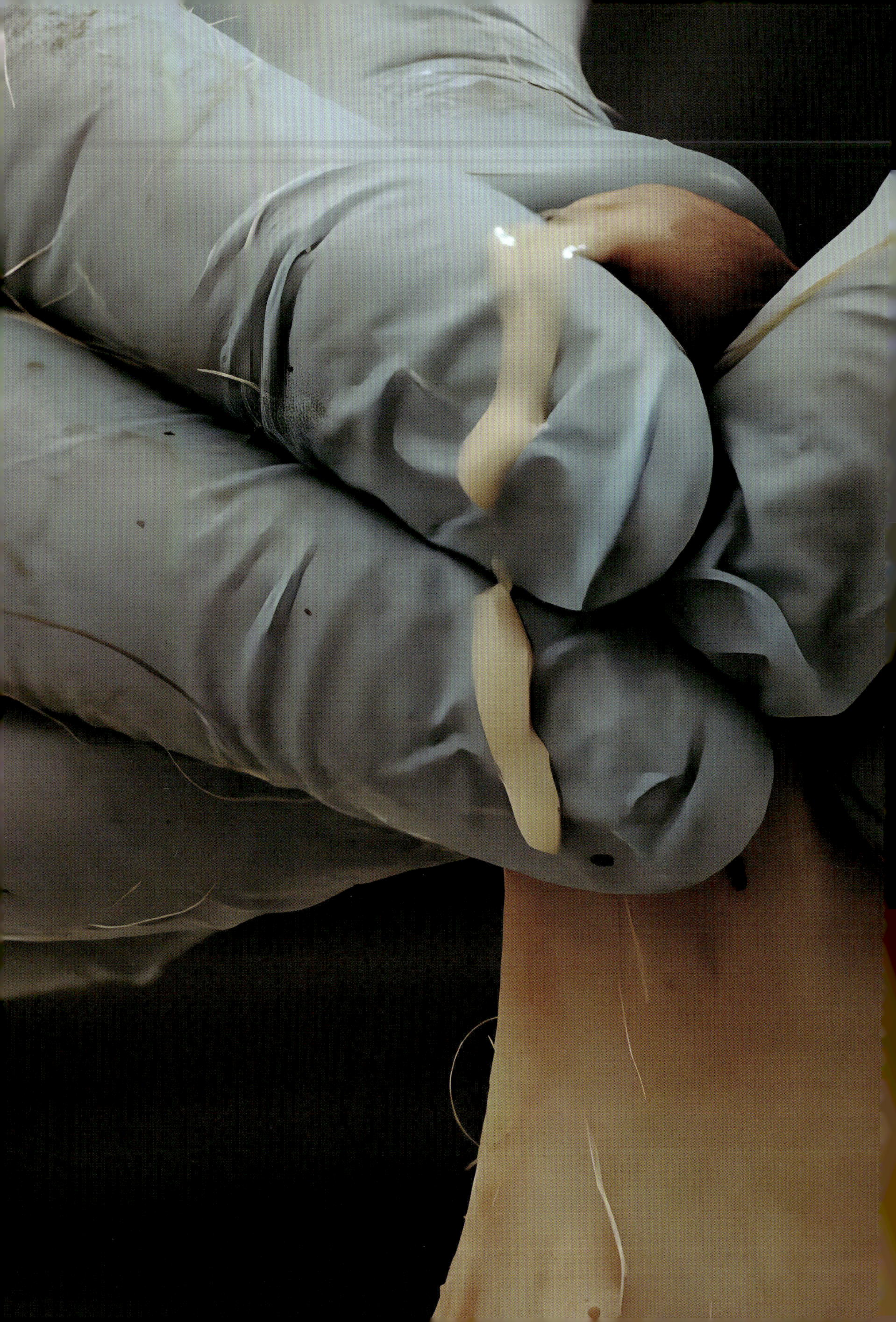

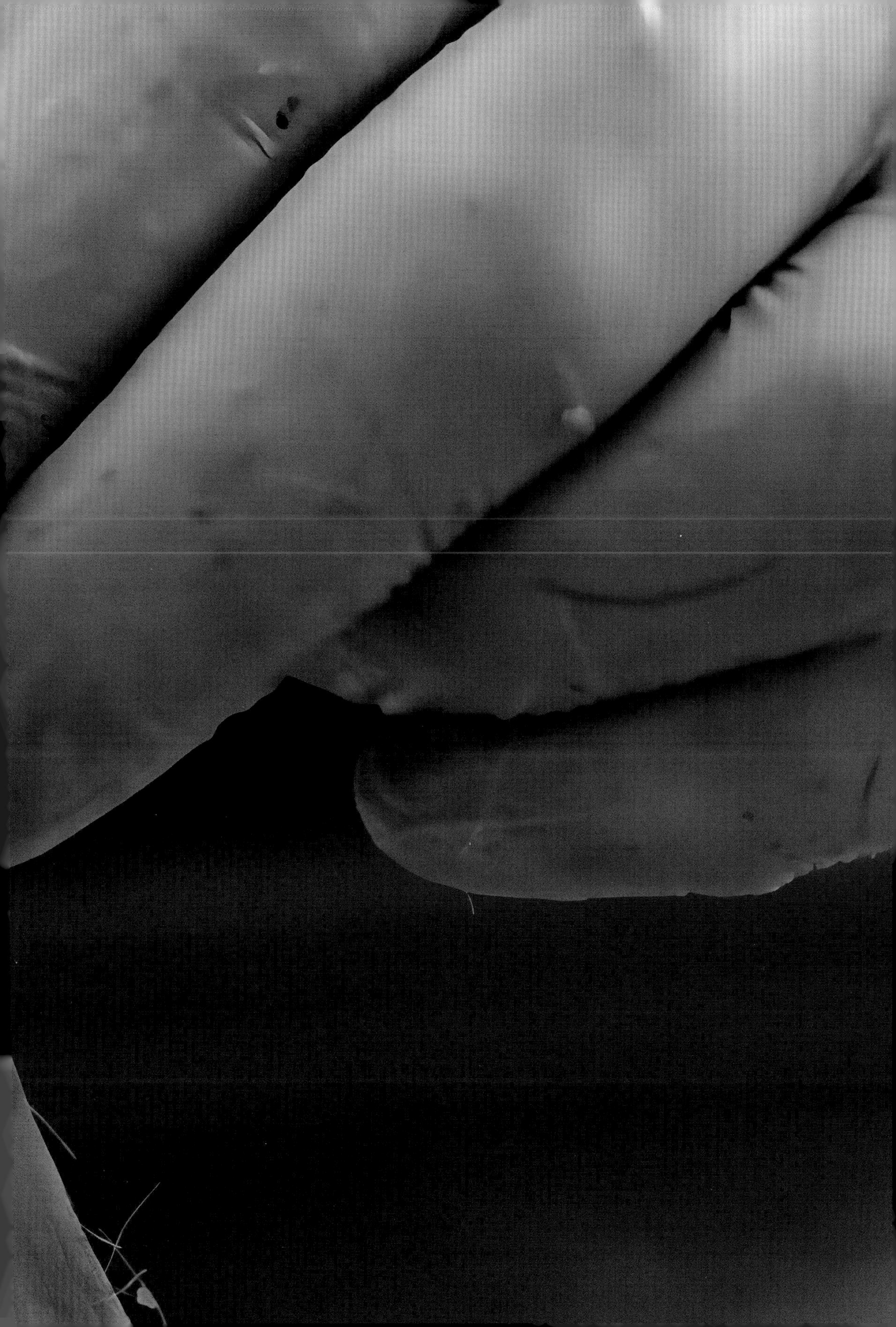

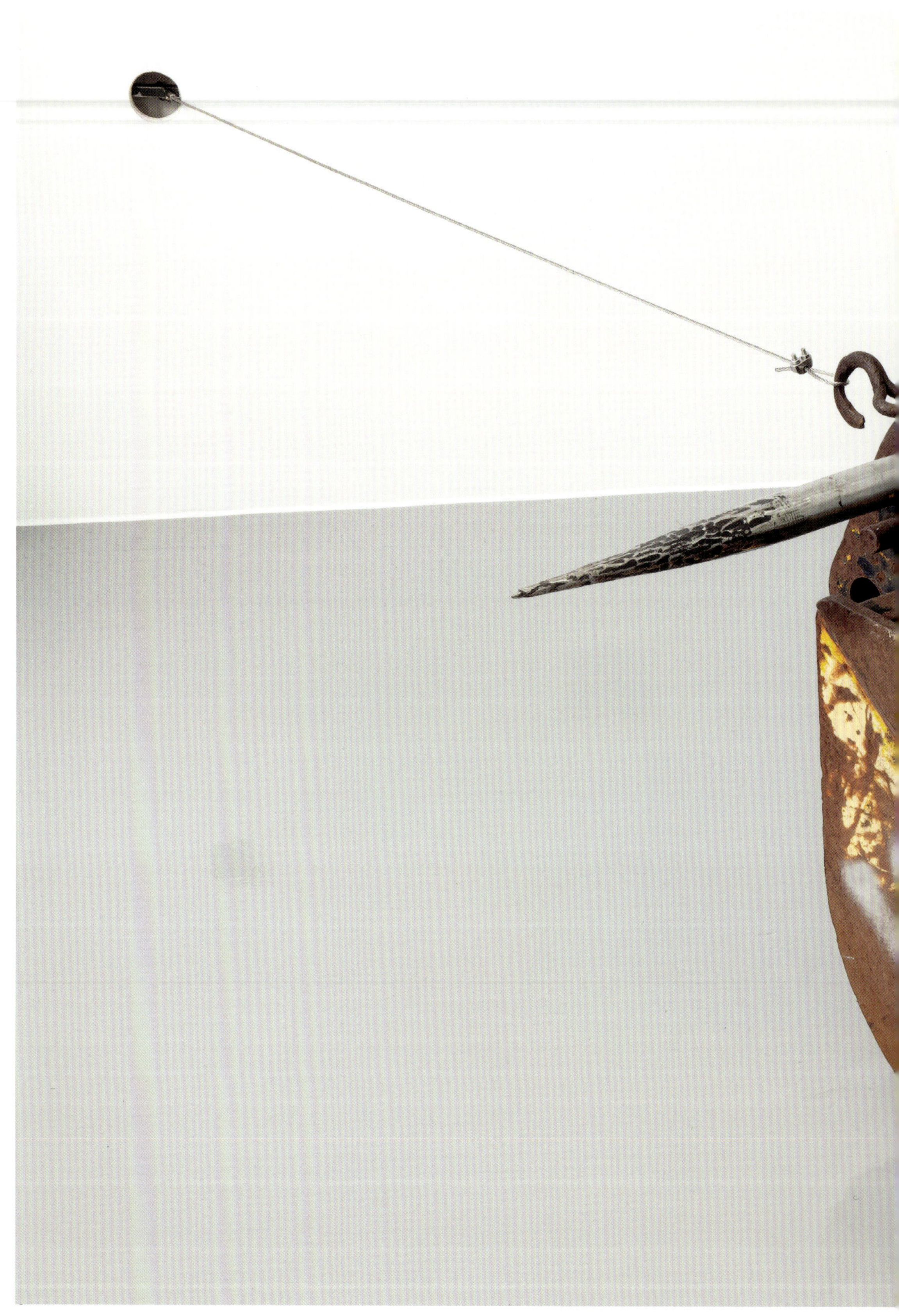

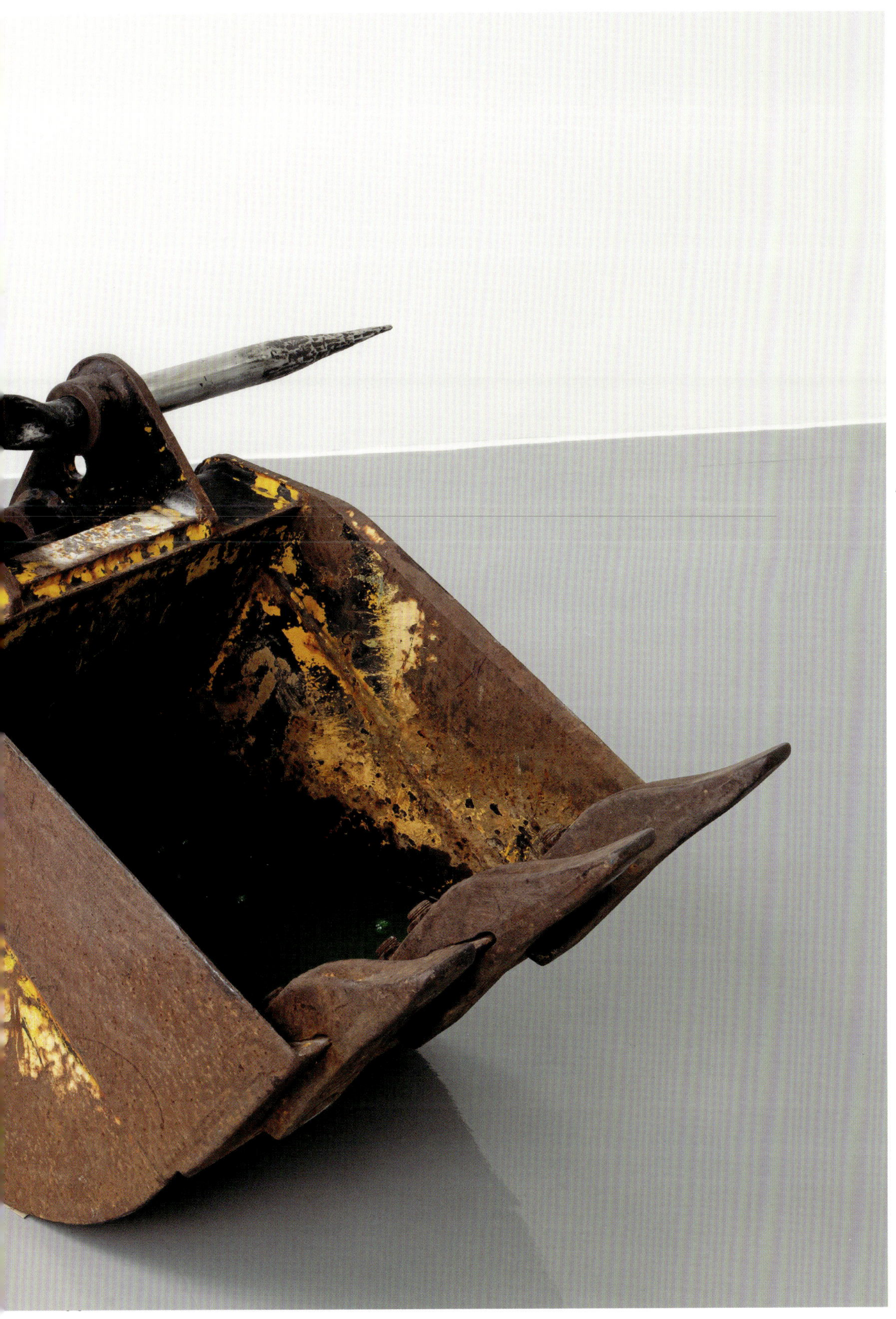

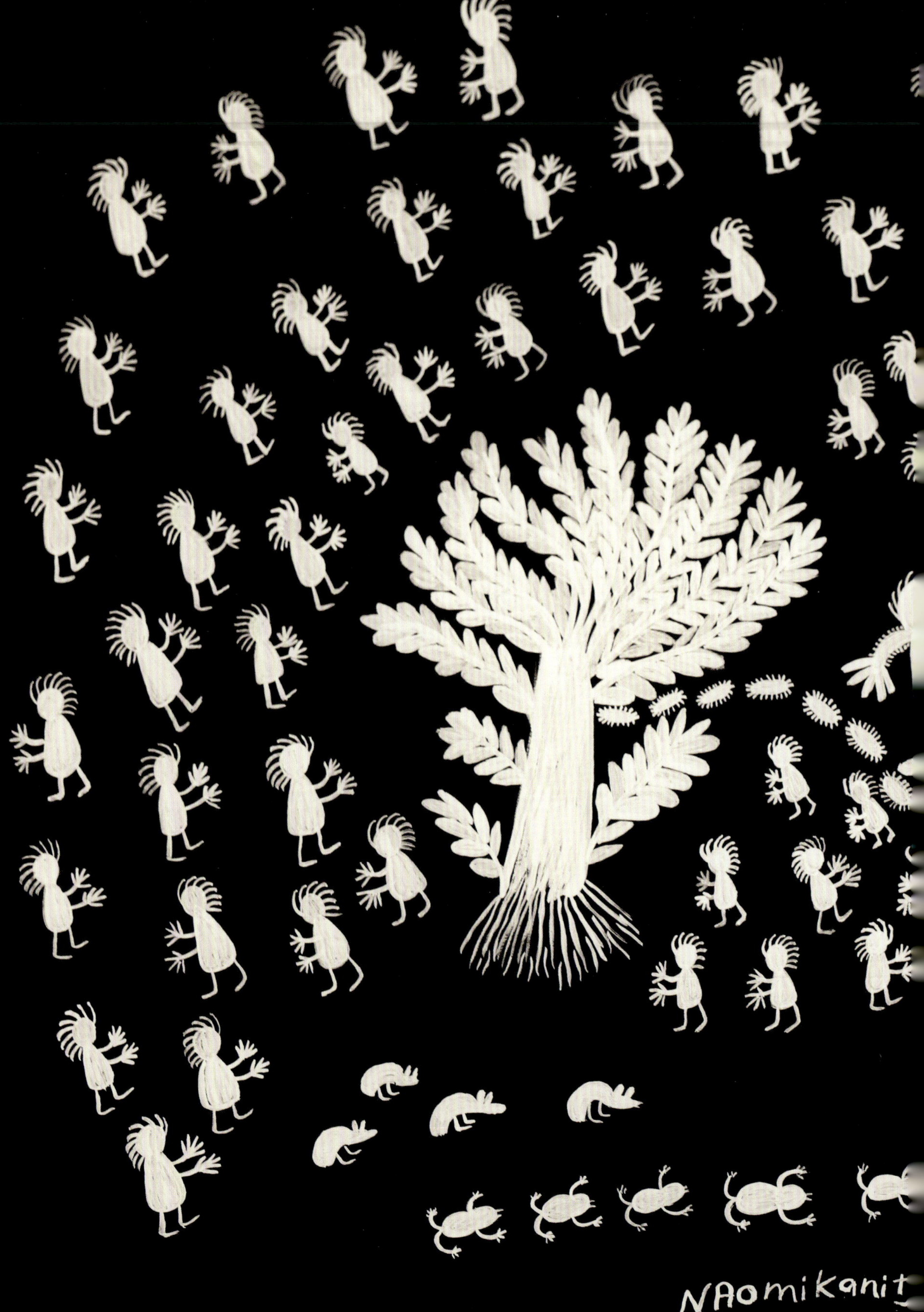
NAOmikanit

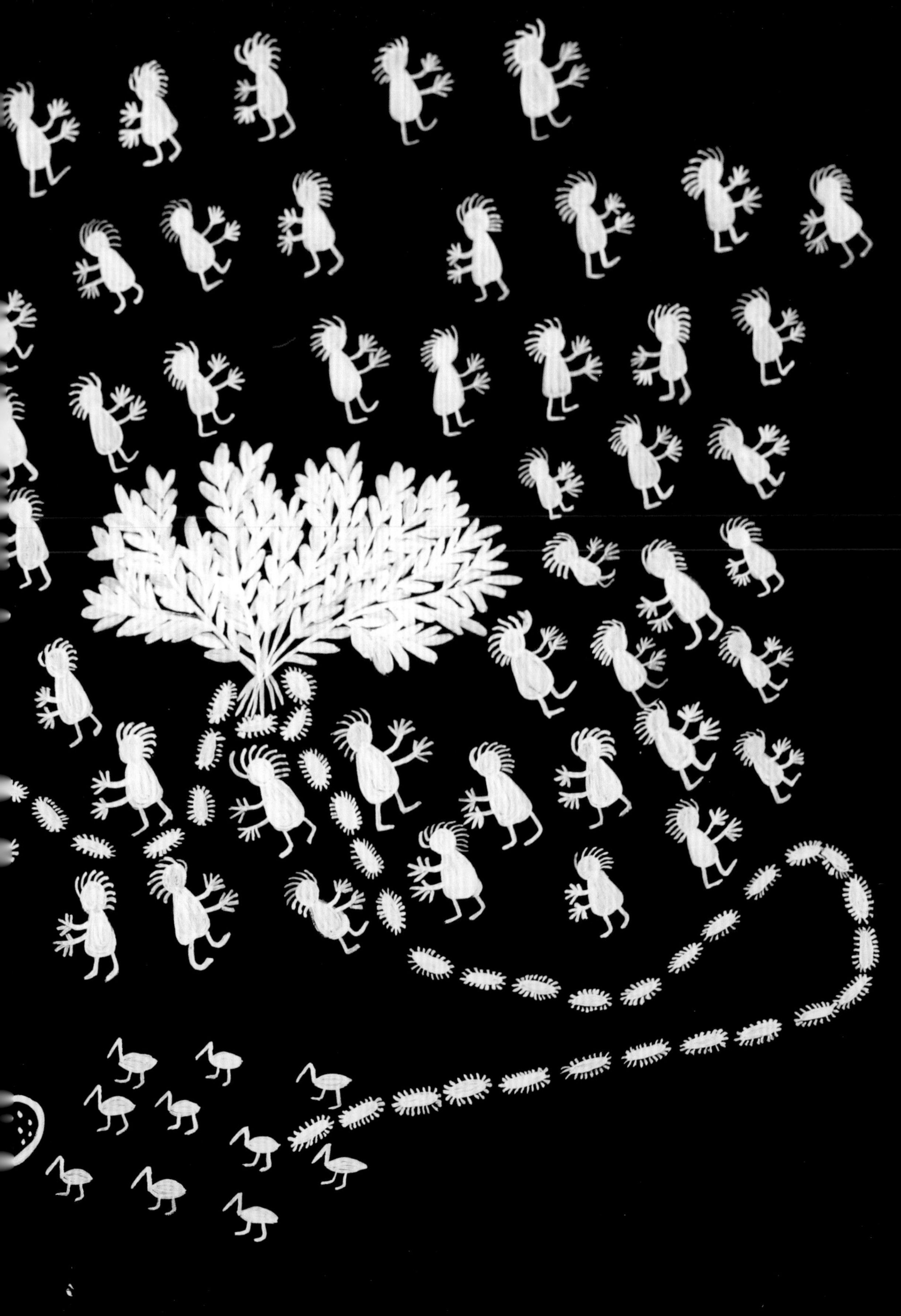

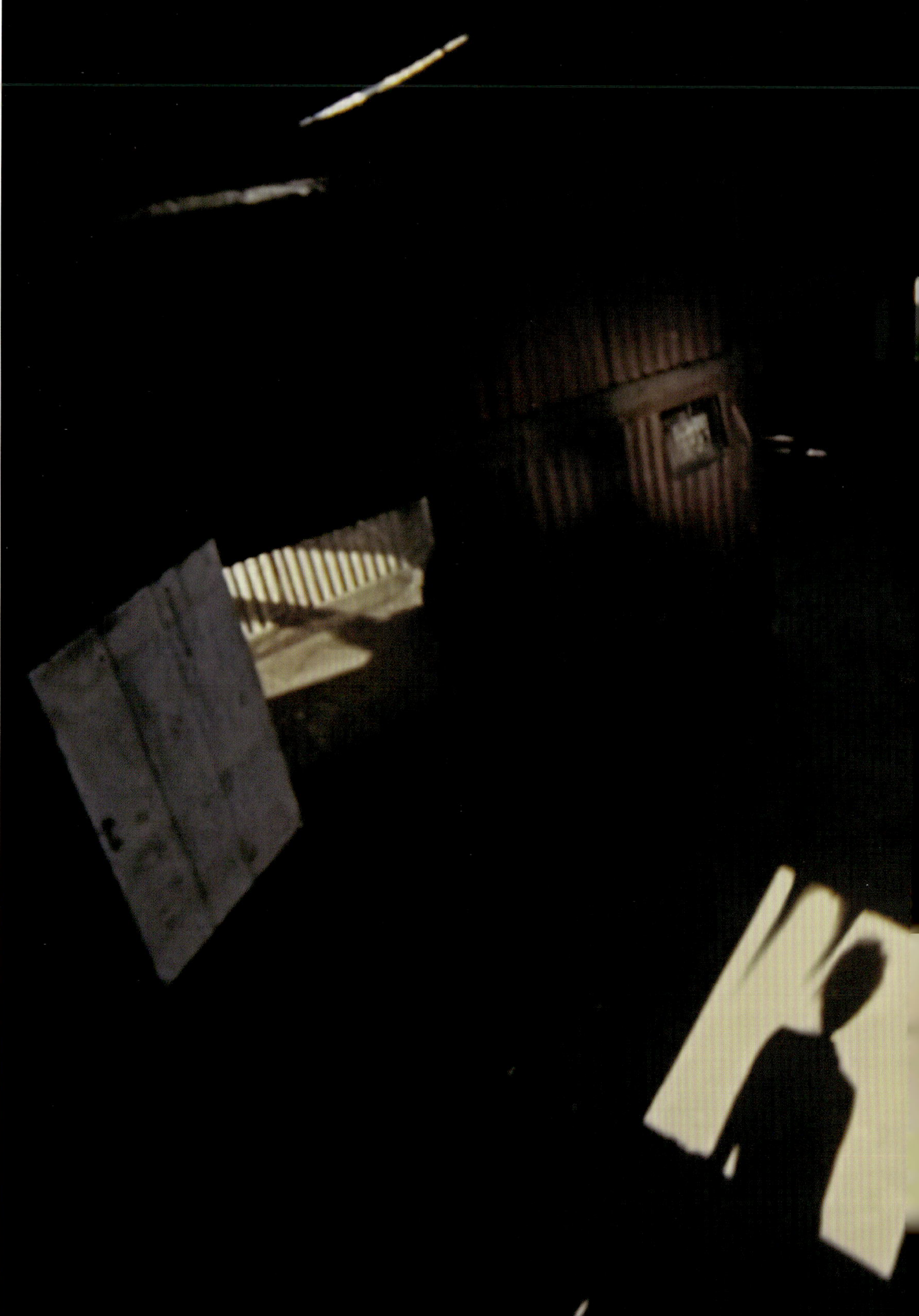

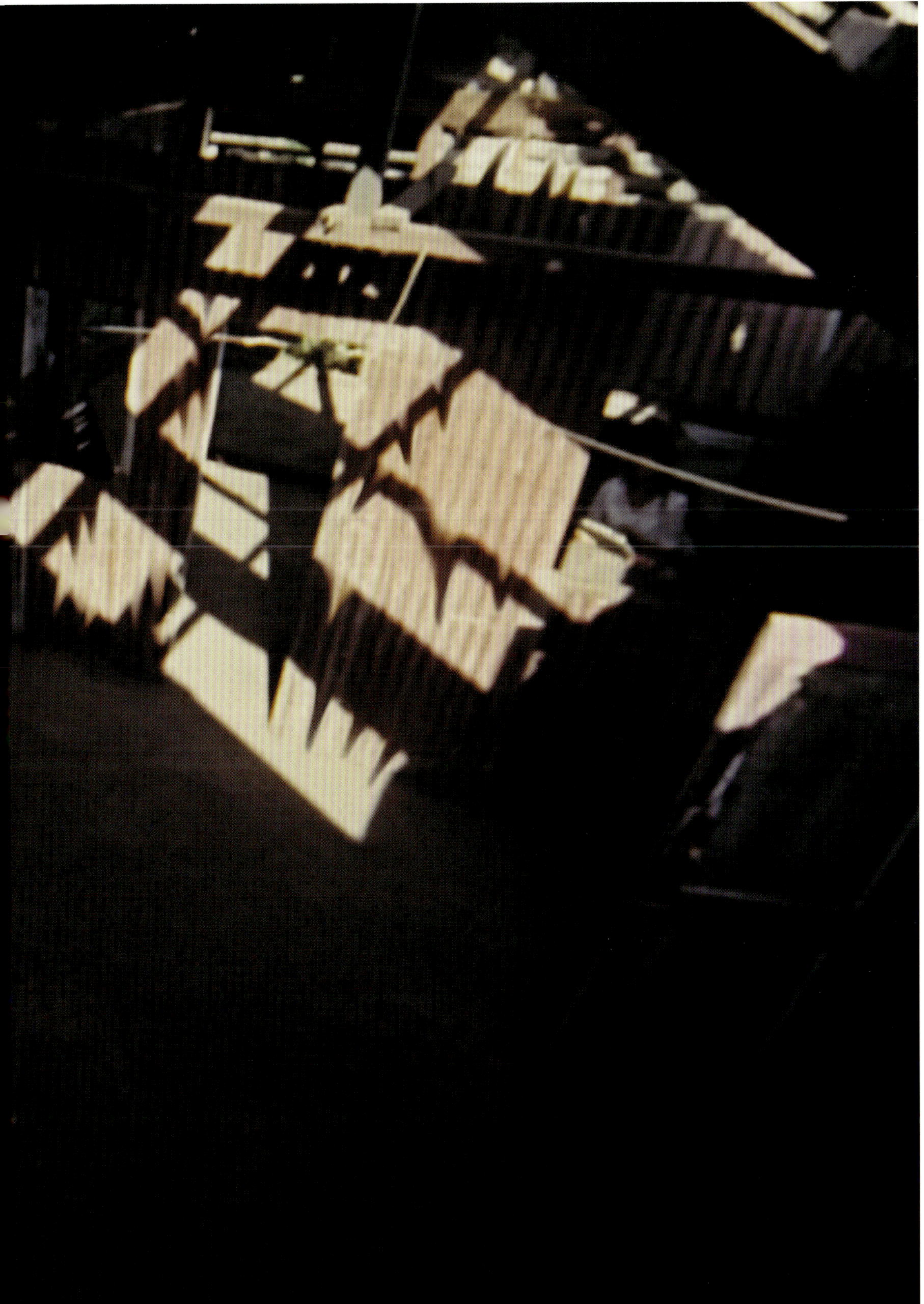

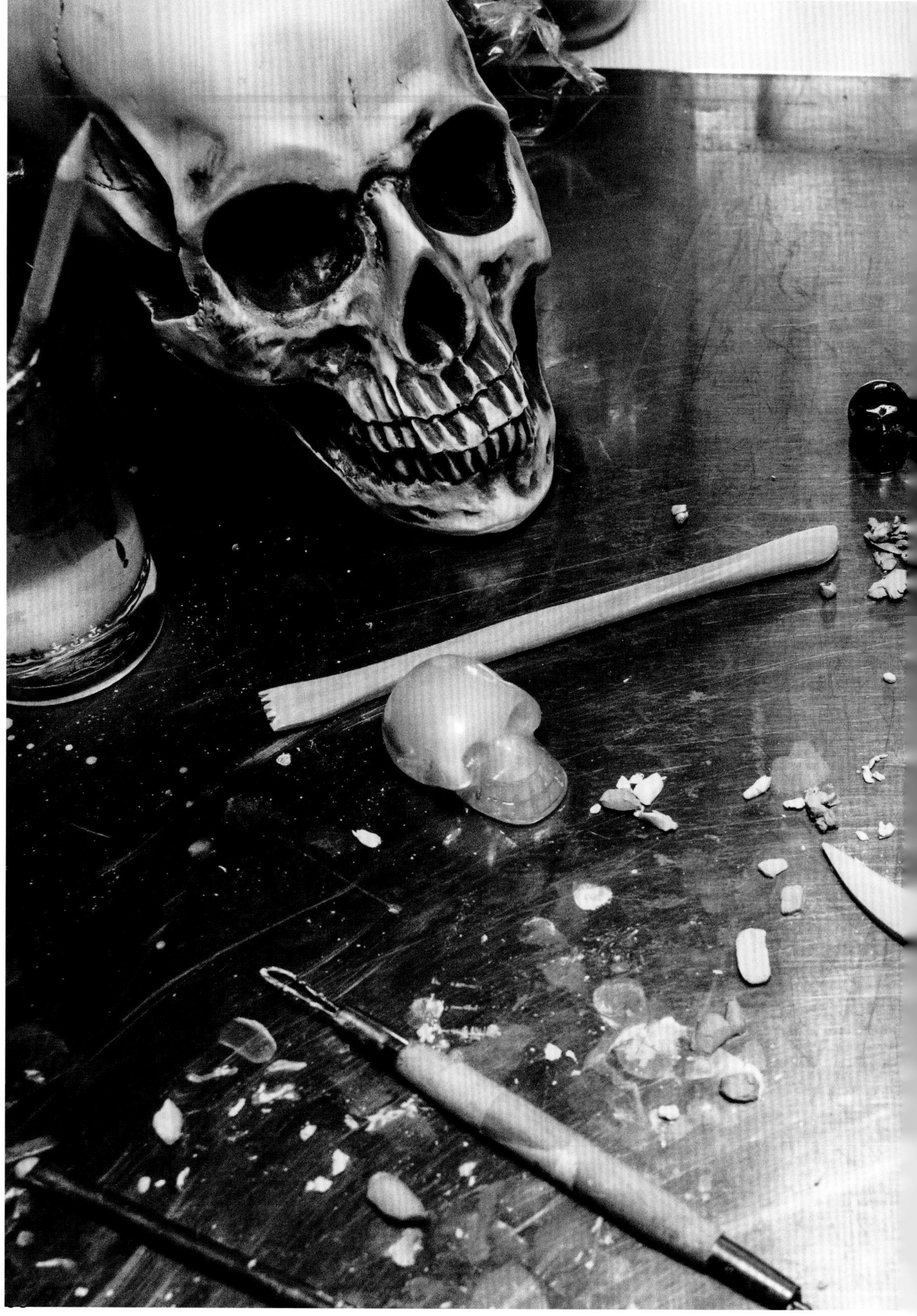

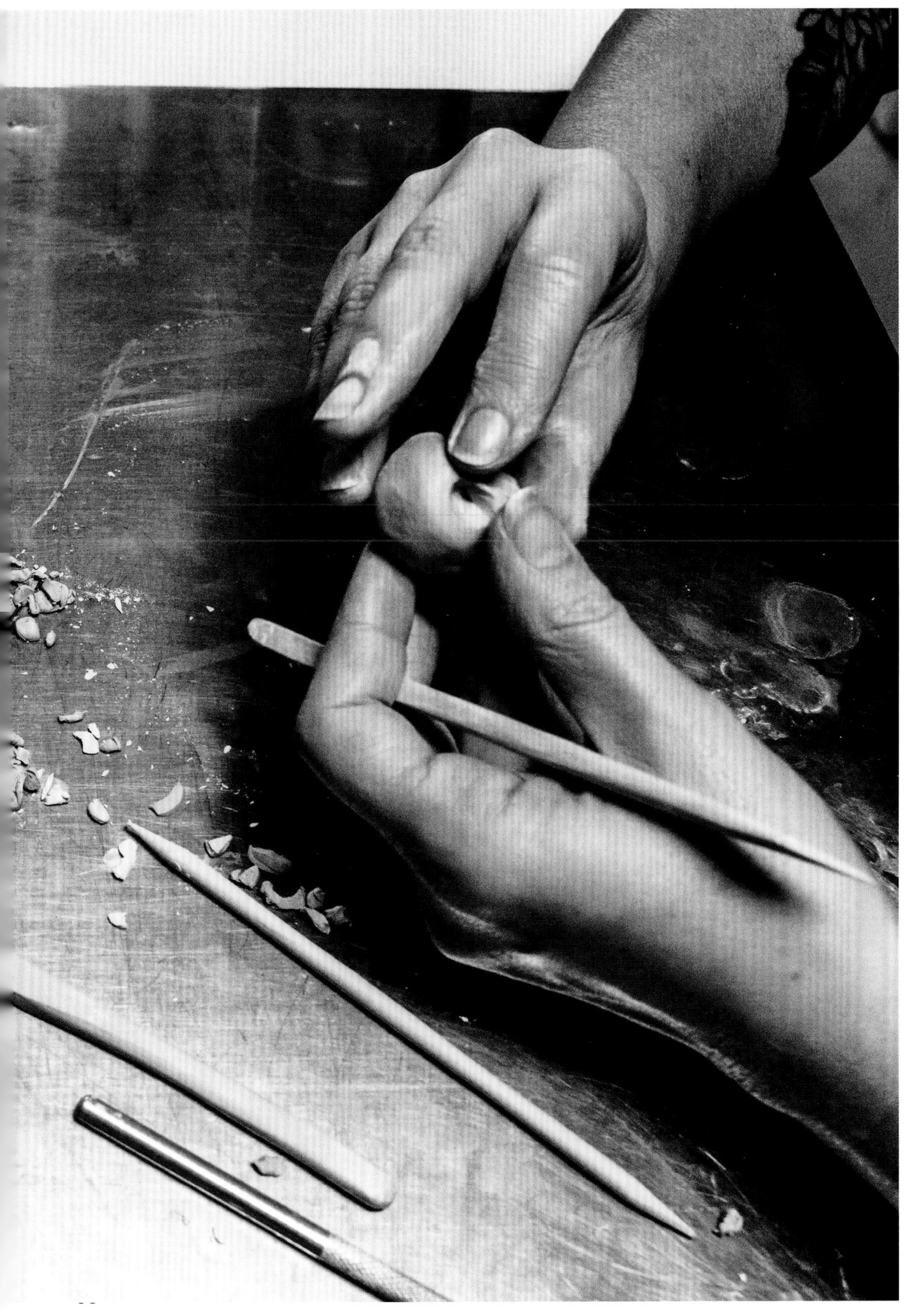

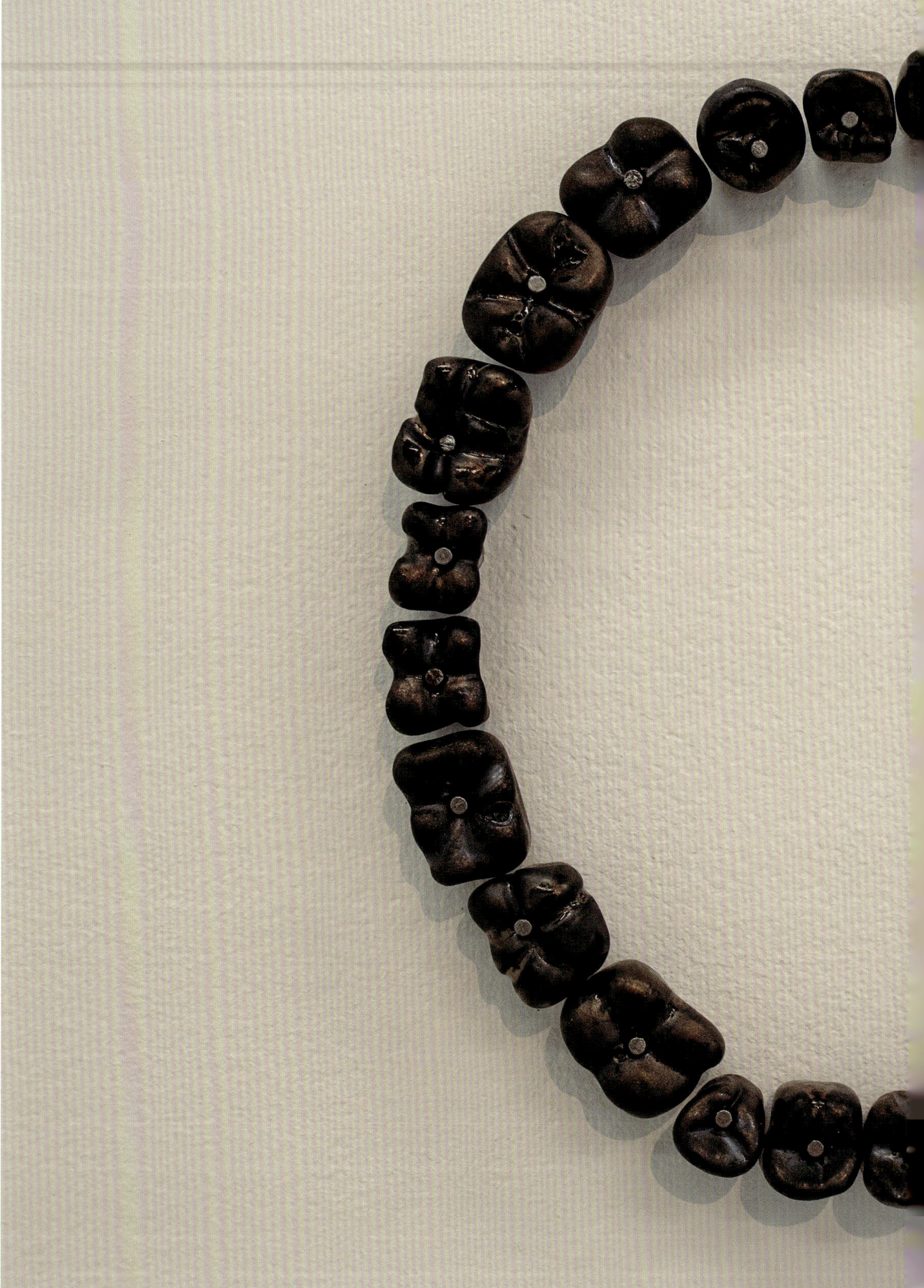

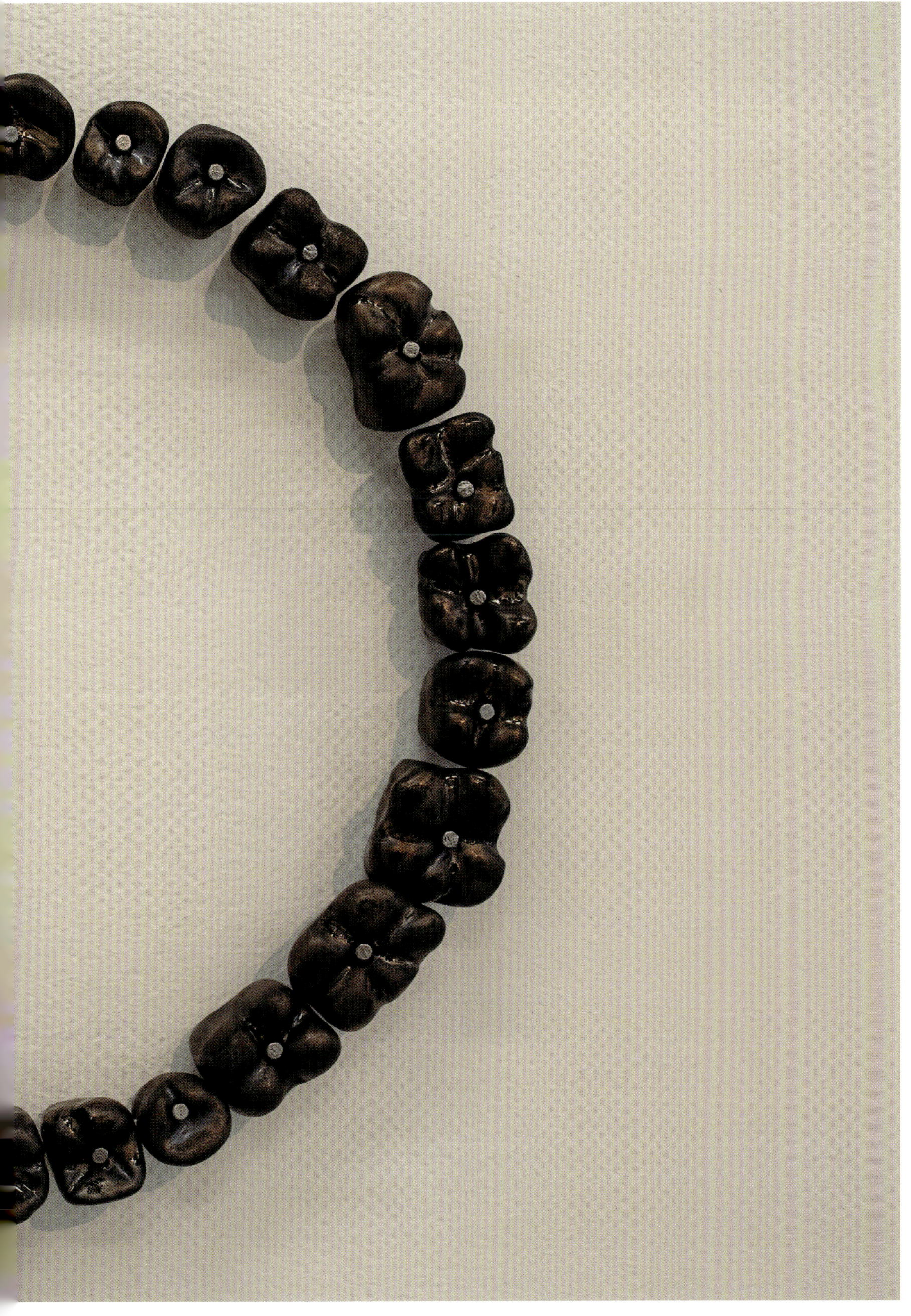

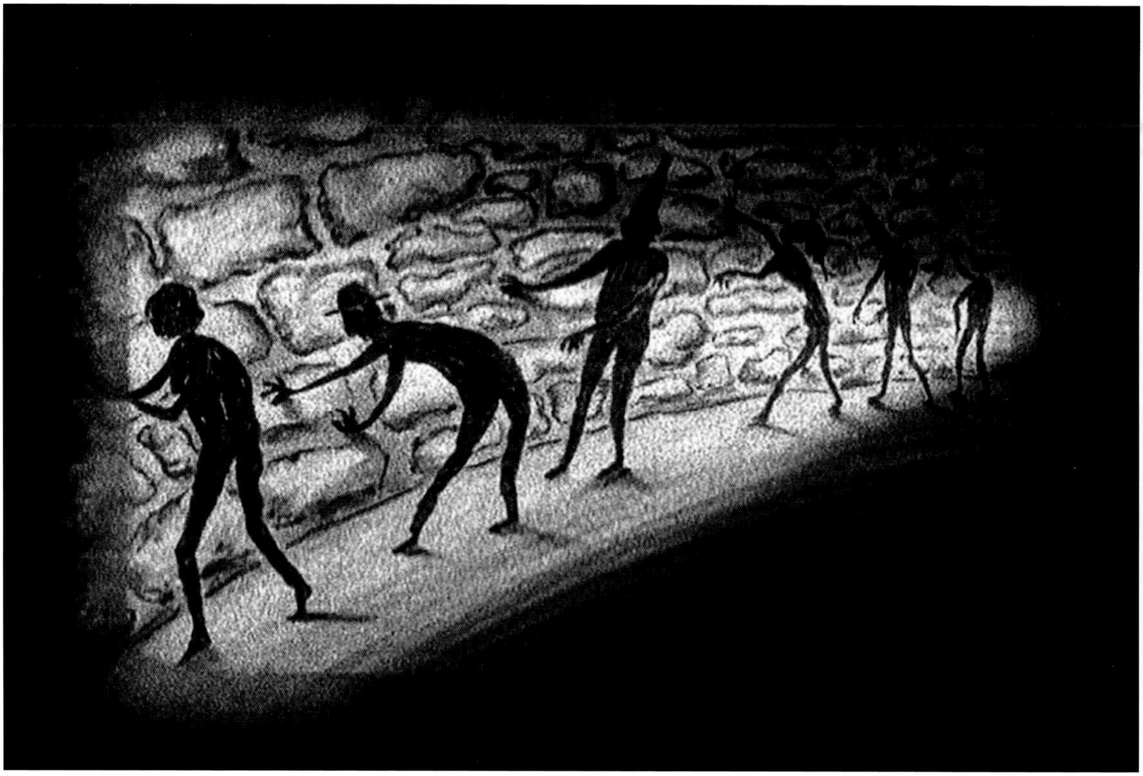

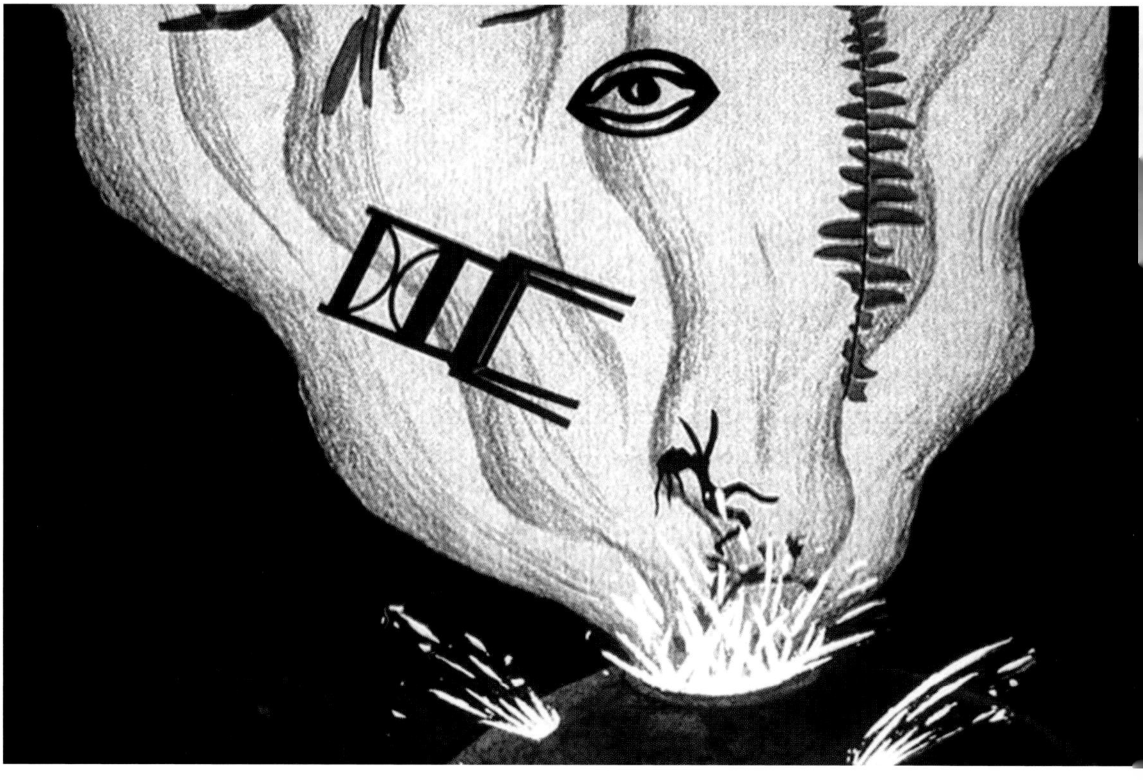

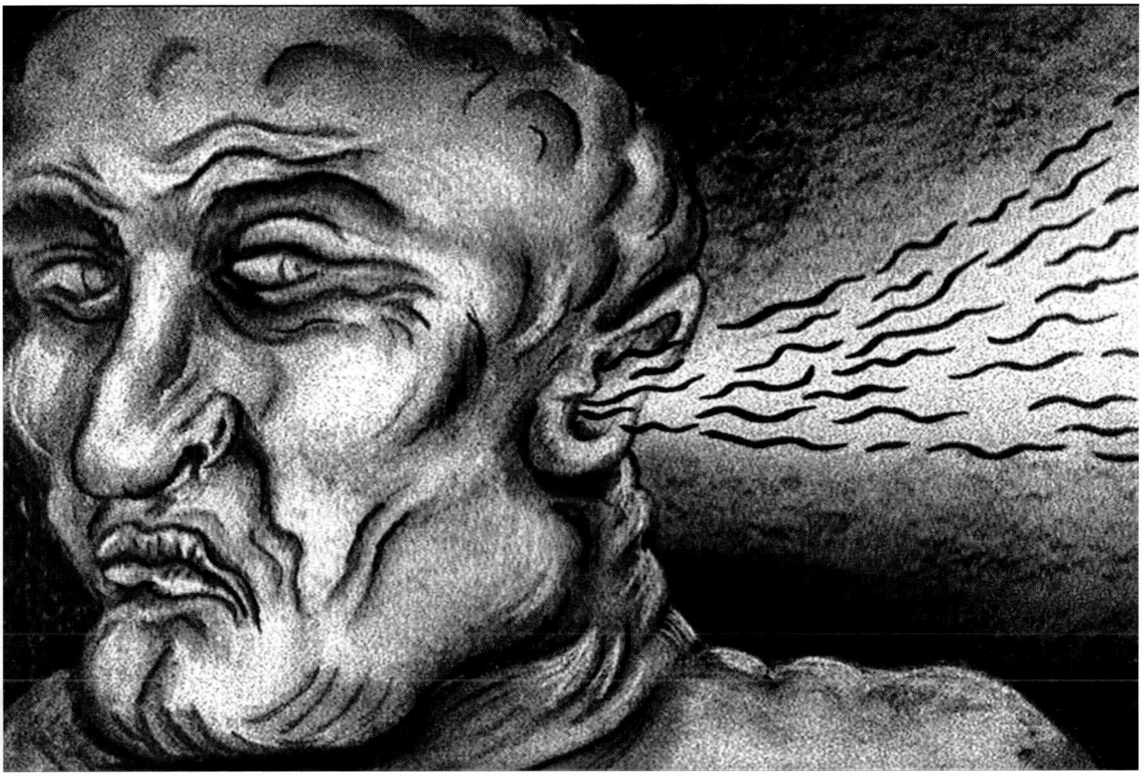

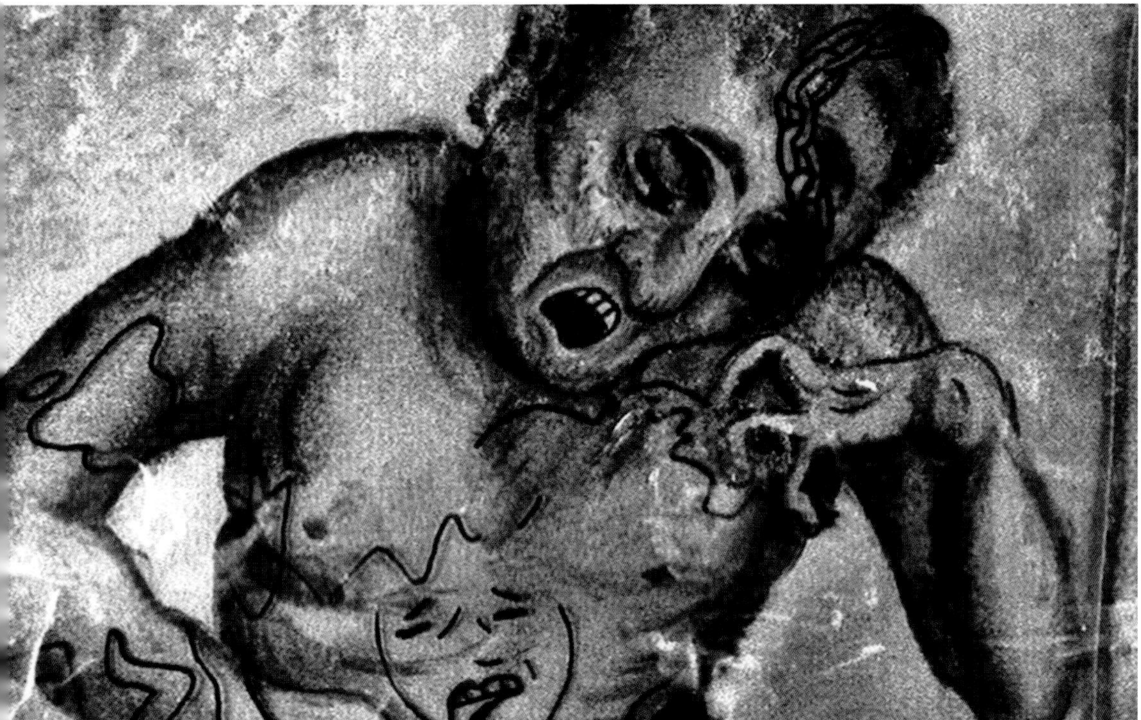

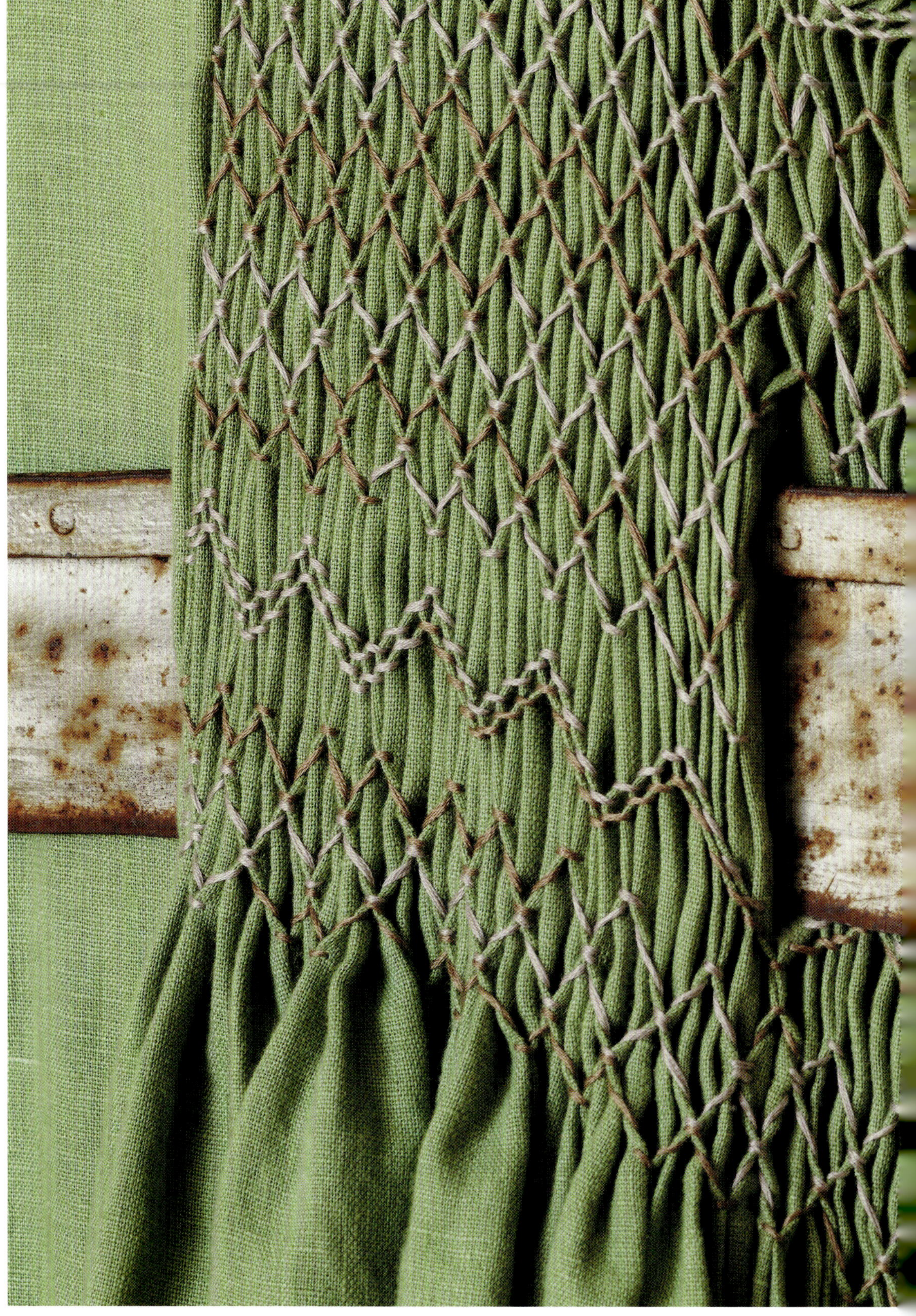

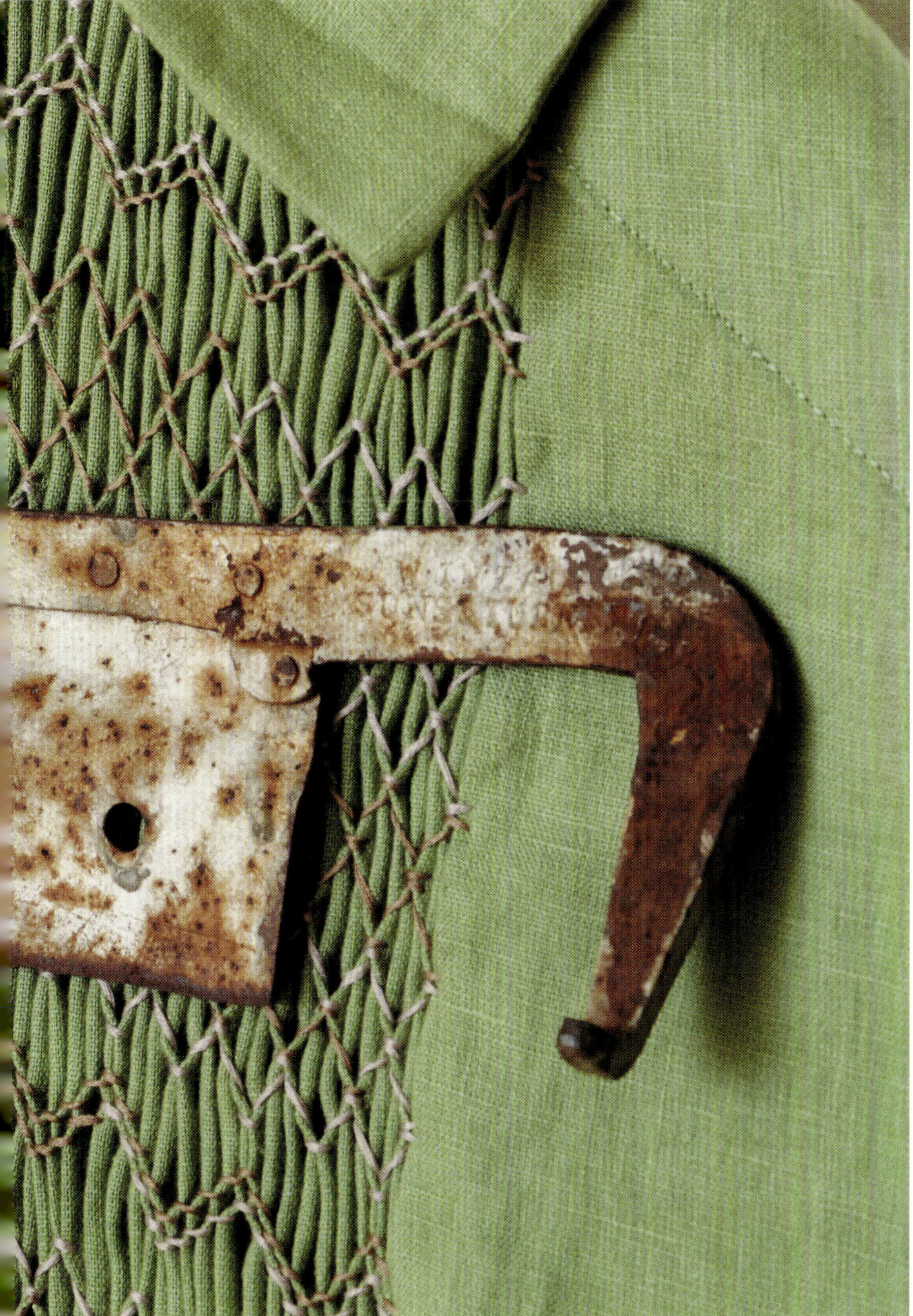

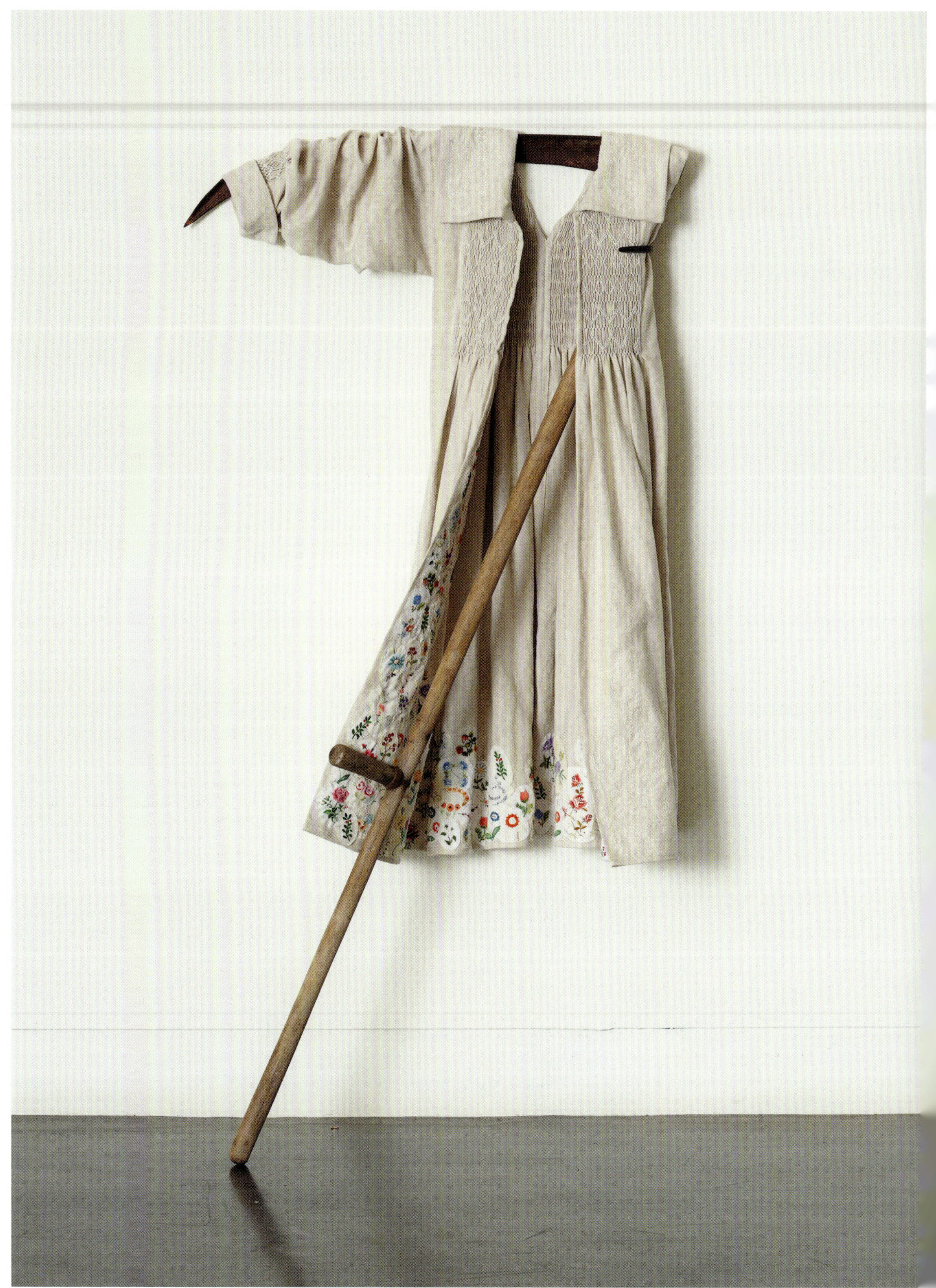

Happy Birthday
Lisa Fuller

Washing my face, I try to banish the wooziness. I splash water over my heated neck with one hand, gripping the edge of the sink with the other. I avoid looking in the mirror. The girl in the tight midriff top and skirt isn't me, I'd been pushed here into this place. This role. By those who said they loved me the most. Who wished me a happy birthday then dropped me at the curb, sending me into the pub alone. I glare at the charm bracelet they'd given me earlier in the day. The lone silver dingo charm winks at me as it swims in and out of focus.

The thought of running hits me. Run from the monster, ignore it and everything I'd ever known. I could do it. But I'd lose my family too.

A face holds me in place. The old woman we'd met that morning, care-worn wrinkles under eyes bleeding despair and rage. Elizabeth, Bett for short. Aunty Bett for young ones like me. The one with the missing granddaughter.

My mother's voice rings in my ears, guiding, judging, like always. *'There is never just a single moment. Just one choice made to reach a path'.*

Not true for me tonight. I don't want to be here. To do this. I have no choice and it will mark me forever. It's my birthday.

Leaving the toilet, I reach out to brace myself. A strong hand grabs my arm.

Startled, I nearly stagger into the wall.

Roland grins down at me, his towering bulk caging me in. 'You okay? Maybe you should get some air', he says, pulling me away from the wall, even as I tried to pull away.

'I'm fine', I try, but it's slurred.

'Don't worry, I got your purse', his brother Seth adds, taking my other arm.

Across the pub, the bartender turns away.

'No', I try again, but my mouth and tongue won't form the words. Only a small croak comes out.

I blink and I'm out the back of the pub, feeling gravel crunch under my staggering feet.

Blink. I'm at a big red Ute.

Blink. Rough hands dragging me into the back seat.

Blink. Black leather beneath me. Men's laughter and the soft buzzing of the engine matches the sound in my head.

Blink. The car is stopped. I'm alone inside the cab. Voices emerge from outside.

I flex my fingers and toes, feeling is returning. My system shakes off chemicals faster than most, one of the few advantages.

'You doubt our ways. This is your history. This is who you are'.

Who I am got me here? Great parenting.

Blink. I'm being man-handled out of the car. Hard fingers are probing and prodding unwelcome places. I jerk away and get dumped on the ground.

'I told you she didn't drink enough', Seth growls.

'She'll be awake, it'll make it even better', Roland giggles.

I retch and they leap away as I roll to my side and empty my stomach. All the better to work the drugs out of my system. I scope the dirt track they've parked the car on, the pitch-black bush all around us. No lights. No people to interrupt us.

We're alone. Not good.

Seth crouches, stroking my charm bracelet before ripping it off and examining it. 'A fucking dingo charm'. He waves it at me. 'You know we used to have bounties on these things? Six pence a scalp, only worth five cents now. Useless things'.

He shoves it into his pocket, then grabs me by the throat.

'Hey, it's my turn to go first', Roland whines.

Seth rolls his eyes, turning back to his brother. 'Rock, paper, scissors?'

They're too distracted with their sick game to notice when I get my feet under me. I sprint toward the closest trees.

'Fuck!'

Feet scramble behind me, but I'm already in the trees. Darting faster, feeling the last of the fuzziness slip away.

'You moron, how much did you give her?' Seth spits.

The night welcomes me, pushing back the doubt and fear of this moment. Not fear for me. Fear for what I will become. Not a girl, not a woman. The monster waits.

My nose picks up a scent, one that shouldn't be here this thick in the bush. I turn to the right, following it down into the gully. Behind me they crash through the brush, noisy elephants. I stay just ahead, making sure to give them glimpses.

Buy us time. We'll be there.

The thought of running pops into my head again. Run and keep running till I hit the next town. Vanish, just how I'd been taught. They'd never find me now that my training was done.

Another face this time. Aunty Bett's granddaughter, Serena. Just nineteen, one year younger than me. In her photo her eyes had sparkled. 'Missing', the cops said. Adult enough to not be a runaway. Troubled home life. Blak. Labels to keep her less than human. So they don't have to care.

Softer sounds float to me, of small bodies barreling through the bush. I catch glimpses of moving shadows. Moonlight occasionally catching soft fur.

My chance to run is gone. I slow down more.

The gully bottoms out into a small gorge with high walls. Probably a long dry creek had carved this space. The moment is coming. If I do this, there's no going back. I'd be like them. A monster.

A body hits me, sending me crashing to the sand. Grit covers my face and hands as a heavy weight forces me down.

'Gotcha bitch', Roland growls. I take satisfaction in his panting.

He flips me over as Seth jogs up, as red-faced as his brother. A mix of sweat, over-exertion and rage. His lips curl in a cruel way.

'Think you're smart', he wheezes, gesturing around. 'You just made it that much easier'.

'Brought us right to our spot', Roland guffaws.

He sweeps his hand out, encompassing the sides of the gorge, up against the rock walls. There's a smell here. One I try not to identify. But my nose screams at me, the sweet decay and gut churning rot.

'The bartender', I puff, 'he saw us. He'll tell them I was with you'.

'He hasn't before', Roland's creepy giggles make Seth chortle.

'See no evil, hear no evil. Speak. No. Evil'. Seth emphasises each word with a step towards me, rubbing his fingers and thumb together to show me how he bought their silence.

He's on me in a moment, straddling my hips and pushing me down.

'Hey', Roland protests.

'Shut the fuck up', Seth snaps, before turning his leering smile back to me, pushing his face into mine. 'Ready for the night of your life, dingo girl? The *last* night of your life'.

I stare into his eyes and know I can't run. It's too late. For me. For him. For all the girls in their graves around us. The monster sits on my chest and knows his prey is cornered.

I force the word out. 'Guilty'.

A low, mournful howl rises through the trees. It bounces off the gorge, haunting and beautiful. Seth sits back in surprise, staring around.

More melancholy howls lift into the night. Shadows shift along the treeline, on top of the cliffs. Growling and yapping barks fill the night.

Seth turns back to me, shocked eyes taking in my calm expression.

Roland cries out, staggering back with a dark shape latched to his calf. Seth yells and tries to rise. I grab him by the throat, rolling till I'm crouched over him, my claws sliding out to pinch his throat. He stares up into my growling face and I smell piss.

Screams fill the night, almost drowning out the growling, ripping and tearing.

'Please', Seth whispers. 'I don't want to die'.

'Did they beg?' I spit. 'How many did you spare?'

Yellow and white shapes glide up, surrounding us. All of them spattered in blood. They wait.

His face twists. 'You're monsters'.

'*We're* monsters?' I lean closer. 'How long did you make them suffer?'

It's my time to join my family, my legacy. My judgement. My choice.

His fear brings me no joy. Hunters respect life, they don't delight in death, even justifiable ones. No one will foul their bodies with this meat.

I strike, spraying the sand in blood. My mouth full of hot metal tang, and flesh.

It's my birthday.

***

Later, I stare around the gorge, rubbing my fingers over my somehow unbroken charm bracelet. I count the shallow impressions in the sand, wondering which one belongs to Serena.

The gorge is free of blood and gore now. All evidence swept clean and cleared away. The cops would get a tip about this place in a few hours. Maybe they'd come look. Maybe we'd have to come up with another way to expose this place, to have these women named and reclaimed by their families. Meanwhile, we'd go see Aunty Bett.

I rub my thumb over the tiny dingo. Monsters. Family. Tradition. Others' words telling me who I am.

These women had been left voiceless, controlled by labels. Abandoned and retraumatised by a system focussed on perpetrators and their rights.

One choice. I had others left. The bartender is due a visit.

Pulling back the clasp, I return the bracelet to my wrist.

Maybe we're the monsters that are needed.

Screams on Screen: How to Monstrously Overspill
Jessica Balanzategui

While the moments often mythologised in best-of lists and reviews are the violent frenzies, kills, and bodily outpourings of blood, bile, and green vomit, the horror film's baroque variations on the scream are at the core of the genre's subversive power. This piercing, tearing, vocal eruption is the sound of terror finally unleashed. It is the sound of the complete collapse of decorum and social mores, and of the piercing of calm 'resilience' in the face of increasingly unbearable adversity.

If a horror film lives up to the promise of the emotive response for which the genre is named, the scream carries from the fictional on-screen world into the real-world of the cinema space. Indeed, some of my most memorable experiences of watching horror movies in theatres involve an unexpected scream from an audience member somewhere in the dark.

One such scream *off* screen occurred at a sold-out screening of Franck Khalfoun's *Maniac*, 2012 , a powerful remake of the grimy 1982 original, by William Lustig. In this version, throughout most of the film the audience is forced to share the first-person perspective of a psychosexually perverse serial killer, Frank. In the bravura opening sequence, we share Frank's point-of-view as he quietly stalks a young woman. The sequence crescendos – almost silently – as Frank creeps behind her through city streets, and finally down the darkened hall to her apartment. As she moves to unlock the door, Frank finally chooses his moment to emerge from the shadows. 'You're so beautiful', he murmurs while wielding his glinting butcher's knife – the archetypal slasher-killer's weapon. As she opens her mouth wide in shock and horror, about to unleash the piercing scream that is the genre's sonic hallmark, the killer purrs sweetly and softly: 'please don't scream'. He abruptly jams the knife through her lower jaw, the blade piercing into her gaping mouth. This violent motion silences the scream just as it was about to burst free, freezing her expression in an anguished wide-open – but mute – gape. Frank redacts the woman's scream and takes her life in the same swift gesture.

At this moment, someone in the audience let out a shocked scream. The jarring sound filled the deadening silence of the on-screen scream. This response was so collectively cathartic that the full-house theatre erupted into raucous applause.

These shared physical eruptions between audience and character crystallise the transgressive catharsis of the horror genre. Far from being *just* the powerless wailing of doomed victims (usually women), the scream unleashes all the terror, shock, rage, exasperation, and *power* contained within the body and mind of the victimised screamer. In *Maniac*'s opening sequence, the killer's act of violently silencing the scream is so disturbing because it steals this power. He must silence her scream, because the piercing force of it would have suddenly made his invisible victim visible.

In her book on the 'unruly' feminist body in art, Lauren Elkin writes of the inherent 'art monster' problem in becoming a woman artist. She recalls that she, along with so many of us, was 'groomed to be appropriate, exacting, friendly and accommodating, as pretty and as small as I could make myself, yet filled with rage at not being allowed to take up more space in the world'.[1] Elkin meditates on how the term 'art monster', encountered in the pages of Jenny Offill's novel *Dept. of Speculation*, surged through her like electricity. For Elkin, the term captures how empowerment is derived from monstruous revolt against marginalisation and repression: 'culture punishes women for being something other than small and silent. Our boundaries have been policed; when we have overspilled them we have been called disgusting'.[2] Monstrousness – becoming *art monster* – 'authorizes women to thwart received ideas about how we – and our art – should be, look, behave'.[3]

Despite – and indeed often *because of* – the womanly 'hysteria' that screaming connotes, the scream vocalises a 'fuck the patriarchy' social power. In this way, women victims become art monsters. In Jennifer Kent's *The Babadook*, 2014, an exhausted, single mother of a difficult child is generally quiet and meek in response to being pushed into society's cracks. While clearly exhausted and exasperated with her claustrophobic life, Amelia smiles sweetly, speaks softly, and sits tight and crumpled so as not to take up space. Like Elkin prior to her art monster epiphany, Amelia makes herself as small as possible for her own self-preservation, but simmers with the rage and frustration of the resultant claustrophobia.

Amelia's gentle compliance is punctured as she drives her son Samuel home after he has been expelled from school. Samuel kicks the back of Amelia's chair, screaming while contorting his body, not afraid to unleash his own rage and frustration. Samuel takes up as much space as his emotions dictate, having not endured the decades of patriarchal constriction that, as Amelia's ways of being in the world suggest, have characterised his mother's confining existence. Reaching her limit, Amelia turns around and screams 'Why can't you just be normal!' This outburst unleashes all her repressed frustration with her maternal entrapment, but also enacts the 'bad motherhood' she so deeply fears lurk deep inside her. Indeed, Amelia's scream triggers only louder screams from her child, and immediate frantic guilt of the mother.

Yet, in the movie's climax, the unleashing of Amelia's guttural scream is what ultimately frees her family. Amelia's scream diminishes the power of the menacing bogeyman, the Mr Bababdook of the film's title, an embodiment of the mother and son's shared trauma as much as he is a supernatural force. Standing tall and broad-shouldered, dishevelled and covered in blood, sweat, and dirt – the very image of a bad mother – Amelia hollers 'You are nothing'. She builds to a forceful scream 'This is MY house. You are trespassing in MY HOUSE.' Amelia wields the crescendoing volume of her scream to make herself big where she once was small. She makes wild, hysterical noise and takes up her space. Through her scream, she overspills monstrously, defiantly, *heroically.*

Another sublime scream resounds in *Possession,* 1981, by Andrzej Żuławski, Anna has decided to leave her husband Mark, and the domestic confinement he has come to embody for her. In the aftermath of their messy separation, Anna undergoes a monstrous transformation. In an arresting long take, she walks through a quiet subway with her groceries. Without rhyme or reason, Anna starts to hysterically laugh, grunt, groan, and contort her body. Dry heaving and writhing, her grunts escalate to a deep moaning then screaming, much like Amelia's empowering, primal vocalisation, which has the power to vanquish monsters. Anna's screaming becomes increasingly deranged throughout this three-minute sequence.

As she unhinges, this screaming powerfully breaks through her feminine façade. Counteracting her gentle appearance in a demure long-sleeved, high-necked blue dress, as Anna screams, her groceries spill, the eggs break, and milk smears all over her body and across the dirty walls and floor of the subway. The mess and grime melds with her saliva and sweat. Finally, an ambiguously strange liquid pours from her own body. Through her unadulterated, uncompromising, and unapologetic screaming in a public place, Anna violently overspills. In the process, she throws aside once and for all her unbearably claustrophobic identity as a beautiful, docile housewife.

This is the power of the scream on screen: to monstrously overspill.

The scream rips through the shackles of decorum that undergird oppressive social structures. It is the sound of the horror movie victim – the archetypal embodiment of a marginalised identity – becoming powerful.

1. Lauren Elkin, *Art Monsters: Unruly Bodies in Feminist Art*, Chatto & Windus/Penguin Books, London, 2003. p 6.
2. Ibid. p 13-14.
3. Ibid. p 14.

Inhabiting the Monster: Kate Millett and *The Basement*
Kier-La Janisse

++++

GRAVELY, GRAVELY
Let me tell you a story now. Of a girl obliterated – spiritually and physically – in a basement in Indiana, and the woman who inhabited a monster to make sense of a senseless crime. It is a story of lateral violence, cyclical abuse, the emotional bonds of patriarchy, but most of all it is a story of obsession. And obsession is a thing I can relate to. Especially an obsession that alienates, as this one does.

In 1979 feminist sculptor, author and spokesperson Kate Millett released a book called *The Basement: Meditations on a Human Sacrifice*. Millet was virtually a household name in that decade, having appeared on the cover of *Time Magazine* in 1970 as a result of the incendiary success of her book *Sexual Politics* published earlier that year. She was immediately catapulted to a prominent leadership position within the women's movement – a position that was unwanted and ultimately stifling, as she reports in her 1974 autobiography *Flying*. Her vilification was equally immediate, even from within the ranks of the women's movement itself, especially once she came out as a lesbian; at that time, homosexuality still seen as disruptive to the movement's overarching goals.[1] As art critic Laura Cottingham wrote, Millett was trapped, 'between hero(ine) worship and character assassination'.[2]

The Basement was quite a different beast from anything Millett had penned before – in content, if not in form. Like *Sexual Politics*, it examined the insidious nature of patriarchal oppression, but its means of doing so was through the graphically violent retelling of a true crime in which a woman and her gang of child recruits tortured, mutilated and ultimately killed a teenage girl named Sylvia Likens. The crime took place over three months in 1965, and it was a *Time Magazine* article the following year that hipped Millett to the crime. Millett, then a visual artist making whimsical 'fantasy furniture' sculptures, was permanently changed after reading it. 'For a long time I made sculpture out of a happiness with form itself,' she wrote in a 1988 essay. 'Then one day in 1966, I came across something in a magazine that changed my life. It also changed my sculpture. Something happened, a devastation of the spirit like the collapse of a building. But the rubble revealed a certain door; perhaps it had always been there.'[3] Its effect would dominate her work for the next fourteen years.

I came to *The Basement* as a true crime aficionado, though it is unlike any true crime book I have ever read. Written in the first person and addressed to Sylvia herself, with substantial chapters written in the imagined 'voices' of both Sylvia and her tormentor Gertrude Banisiewski, using an unfiltered stream of consciousness style, *The Basement* is a hybrid work of true crime, feminist scholarship, memoir and experimental fiction that decides halfway through to dispense with relaying the facts of the case and to focus on the imagined interior lives of its participants.

And this is where my interest lies, because this is where things get muddy and murky, where the author explores dangerous ethical terrain in service to illuminating a greater truth, and sacrifices a part of herself in doing so. It is vulnerable and confrontational. There is no objectivity here, only obsession. And that greater truth is ultimately elusive, leaving only the painful evidence of the obsession itself.

I HAVE BEEN SCARED A LONG TIME ABOUT A LOT OF THINGS

'That you endured it at the hands of a woman, the hardest thing in the fable, that too. Who else would be so fit to shatter the woman-child?'[4]

Gertrude Baniszewski was a 37-year-old single mother of seven children, who was herself a survivor of domestic abuse. She took in the teenaged Sylvia Likens and her sister Jenny as boarders because the $20 a week it promised would theoretically feed her starving family, who – as has often been remarked upon – had only one spoon to share between them. Gertrude scraped by with odd ironing jobs, but her repeated respiratory ailments often knocked her out of work for long stretches. She quickly came to resent that the Likens girls were her meal ticket, and punishments in the house – often meted out by Gertrude's 17-year-old pregnant daughter, Paula – were increasingly focused on them. Eventually it was just Sylvia, who became for Gertrude – and by extension the household of children – the cause of everything wrong with their lives. In their minds, every obstacle, every loss, could somehow be traced back to Sylvia. She became so despised as to be dehumanised, made into an object, a doll, a punching bag, sequestered in the basement with no bed or toilet.

'To be feminine, then, is to die,' writes Millett, 'The voices of contention and derision never silent, condemning the victimised to an endless repetition of an ancient implacable fate. Always afraid that the answer to the grand question will be that we invite it, deserve it, court it, permit it. And the conclusion to the two riddles of the basement – why did they do it, why did she let them – will be only another confirmation of all the older annihilating writs: the official theories of female masochism…'[5] She points to the fact that Gertrude was smaller and weaker than Sylvia, even in Sylvia's most malnourished state.

In November of 1978, Millett gave an advance reading from *The Basement* at the San Francisco International Poetry Festival. She spoke of Gertrude's behavior as 'a very obscure, inverted mirror of patriarchal assumptions'.[6] Though they were both women, and thus subject to the same cultural violence and societal oppression, within the walls of the house at 3850 E New York Street, Gertrude sat atop the hierarchy and she wielded that power as it had always been wielded against her. 'That women are their own worst enemies should come as a surprise to no one', wrote Lillie Gross in a contemporaneous review of *The Basement*. 'They have developed the characteristics common to those who suffer minority status and a marginal existence. They hate and reject themselves'.[7]

THEY GOT A WORD FOR GIRLS LIKE ME

'I am a prostitute and proud of it'.[8]

These were the words they carved into Sylvia's abdomen in the last week of her life. Sylvia's sexual identity – however fabricated it may have been, by Gertrude and the others – was the cause of her murder. No matter that the autopsy confirmed her virginity and that testimony relayed her naivete about the subject. She was cast out because she represented something they could not have – one reviewer of the book described that simply as 'hope' – and yet she was rendered abject. At her reading of *The Basement* at the San Francisco International Poetry Festival, Millett introduced the book as examining 'the ultimate meaning of sex in our culture, that you could die for it', asserting further that 'the end of modesty is mutilation'.

Millett's haunting by this case manifested in several earlier works, all involving the central image of the cage: *The Trap* (1967 – an image of which appears on the cover of *The Basement*'s first edition); *No* (1967); *Situations* (1968); *Terminal Piece* (1972); *Small Mysteries* (1975) and finally *The Trial of Sylvia Likens*, the first to directly name the case and refer to its facts and participants. Each of these pieces focused on Sylvia's experience of imprisonment, her isolation and denial of humanity, and each fueled the seething rage that emanates from the pages of *The Basement*. To Millett this is not just a microcosmic study of a universal problem, though that is how she positioned it and justified its graphic depictions of violence. Having lived with these details and thoughts and imagery for fourteen years at the time of writing *The Basement* – and having been involuntarily institutionalised herself in 1972 (though this was kept quiet until the publication of her book *The Loony-Bin Trip* in 1990) – it's undeniably personal.

Throughout the book Millett's language is angry and forcefully crass. Responding to the courtroom analysis of the state of Sylvia Likens' vaginal area, she spits: 'A dry fuck indeed. A kick. But no entry by hand or mouth or tongue or penis. Sexuality without sex. Pure ideology. Ideas about sex, notions, values, superstitions, feelings, hatreds, fears – everything about sex but the thing itself; the act of it of such powerful taboo that one resorts to violence, to sadism, to any and every brutality to avoid it. To stamp it out'.[9]

Most of the kids are not even old enough to know what sex is, or why it is shameful, or why it summons such sadistic hysteria in Gertrude, but they are gleeful about the permitted savagery all the same. They are happy to poke, kick and burn the hidden places on Sylvia's body, even if they can't identify the sensations it gives them.[10] Even Jenny, Sylvia's younger sister, laughs when Sylvia is forced to shove a coke bottle up her vagina. But it's the laughter of self-preservation: 'it exults before the example of its own fate escaped'.[11]

But Gertrude knows what it means, at least, in Millett's retelling of events. She must know.

BEING GERTRUDE

'You are outside Gertrude now. Or Sylvia. The screams, the shouting. Now project the image again. A picture of a hand wrapped around hair'.[12]

The most uncomfortable parts of *The Basement* are not the extensive passages of graphic physical and sexual violence, but those chapters that assume the fictionalised voices of Gertrude and Sylvia. Millett slips in and out of 'character', slides between them, sometimes catching herself doing it. She's like a medium, channeling the dead. It is a biographical transgression that feels treacherous. But these are also the bravest moments of the book because it's where Millett lays everything bare – if not strictly revelatory concerning Gertrude's thought processes (which we can never know), then certainly concerning Kate Millett's. It would seem sensational if not for such a noble purpose, crossing over into the darkness to pull Sylvia Likens back into the light.

A victimised teenage girl is the obvious point of identification for any woman who has some residual trauma hanging around; when Millett slips into Sylvia's voice it is very similar to her own prepubescent voice in her earlier autobiography *Flying* (1974), right down to the masturbatory musings. 'Sylvia I could understand immediately', she offered, 'it took me the whole book to figure out Gertrude'.[13] I wonder if it's frightening to Millett how easily she can become Gertrude. Unlike Sylvia, she goes into Gertrude's voice with confidence and full force. The anger is there, it is accessible and familiar. In speaking about the book Millett has all the anger that Gertrude does not dare show in public. The women's movement brought that anger out into the open, refused to apologise for it. But feminism didn't – still doesn't – tend to find people like Gertrude. Their anger remains unarticulated, and its expression often distorted.

Millett imagines that Sylvia presented for Gertrude a direction; even a vocation: 'Perhaps the coming of Sylvia has contributed this much – that it helped her to see her course, as much as any fortuitous occurrence, any stimulus can clarify the imaginative or emotional process, and will assist, at least in the beginning, to release the repressed desire and intuitive choice which remained suspended before'.[14] Through Sylvia she will banish repressed sexual desire through its transmutation into violence. This ritual implementation of scapegoating, through which Sylvia will be sacrificed, having absorbed all the sins of the larger group, will spiritually elevate both Sylvia and her tormentors (even Sylvia's corpse was found in a beatified state, freshly washed and arms crossed like a saint).

When people write about true crime they tend to use words like 'unimaginable', 'unfathomable', 'unspeakable' – but not Millet. She can imagine it, and she speaks it. The ease with which Millett glides into the vulgar perspective of the killers – 'that little cunt, she deserves it' – shows how much violence is a part of the world she inhabits, for better or for worse. Her embodiment of Gertrude – from the rush of spontaneous orgasm upon seeing bloodied young buttocks lashed repeatedly to the transmutation of this abusive ritual into a sacred and magical act allows Gertrude to romanticise the torture of the girl, articulating it in a way Gertrude would never dare speak aloud, or even think within the hidden confines of her own head. And through this trajectory of punishment, culminating in the searing of text on Sylvia's belly, the desired becomes abject: 'The words themselves were the crisis point', Millett offers, 'the orgasm that purifies because it produces disgust'.[15]

Millett has to fabricate Gertrude because Gertrude gives us nothing. On the stand, the 'wraith-like' woman is brilliantly evasive, no hint of an admission, or even an emotion. She throws her own kids under the bus. She is so resilient in her denial of any wrongdoing that by presenting blankness she instead became a cipher, and allowed for interpretation and mythification, just as Sylvia's suffering became hagiographic in the retelling. And Sylvia, in Millett's imagining, rationalises her own acquiescence as a feeble attempt to win Gertrude's affection, perhaps 'to be loved most of all'. This is fiction, but it is fiction based on historical patterns of behaviour, however frustrating and sad. In the end 'Sylvia' acknowledges the inverted bond that will fuse the two women forever: 'I did become your center after all, but I got it all wrong'.

WHAT DOES IT MEAN THAT YOU DIED?

The publication of *The Basement* signaled a few things. Most notably, it mercifully laid to rest Kate Millett's obsession with the Sylvia Likens case. Her artwork and activism continued to centre issues of incarceration, but the Sylvia Likens case in particular was no longer informing – or dictating, as any obsession does – the direction of her work.

But also, being released at a time when the women's movement was especially fractious and contentious, and tightly focused on the crisis of male predation of women, it invited predictably divided responses. 'This crime, it seems, has haunted Millett ever since she read about it in *Time*, and now she's let her obsession with it run on for 300-plus pages of angry incoherence', moaned *Kirkus Reviews*, 'Millett did no leg work, interviewed nobody, and never got past the surface of this ghastly mystery. An insult to responsible feminist writing'.[16] Kathleen Barry (author of *Female Sexual Slavery*, published the same year as *The Basement*) likewise questioned the moral responsibility of the author, writing in *New Women's Times Feminist Review* that, 'One needs to ask why a feminist would choose a case of violence against a female child by a female adult care-taker... we do obscure the pervasive condition of male violence when we highlight the female criminal... I fear that all the concerted feminist action mobilised now against male cultural violence will be challenged by using the lesser incidence because of this book'.[17] Barry notably takes issue with there being no larger societal pattern through which the case can be generalised, and that as an anomaly, delving into its sordid details can help no one.

Even among those who praised the book for its courage in initial reviews, there appeared frequent use of the adjectives 'repetitive' and 'irritating'. Which seemed very much the point; abuse is repetitive. And if Kate Millett's imagination places her among those inside the house, then perhaps this portion of the book's audience parallel the neighbours who listened to Sylvia scream for months on end and were merely 'irritated'.

Still, Millett's approach was not without its champions. 'It is the first feminist treatment I have ever seen of a sensational crime committed by one woman against another, analysed and documented from a feminist perspective', wrote Juana Maria Paz in *Big Apple Dyke News*. 'We have marched, ranted and raved, made speeches, and written volumes on the violence done to us by men. But what about when a woman leads the reign of terror and what does that say about us, or to the movement?'[18] And as Donna Dinovelli wrote in the *Hartford Courant* – clocking the similarity to *Cinderella* and its wicked stepmother – 'it's a fairytale that doesn't have a happy ending because it never ends. Its implications go on forever'.

Today, female predators are still understudied, but their increasing visibility in scholarship is no longer seen as counter to the advancements of feminism. We have entire television series focused on 'women who kill,' and the fanbase for the popular true crime genre is overwhelmingly female. But *The Basement* still stands apart as a singular work. And this is not because of its forensic documentary detail but because of the angry voice at its heart, desperately reaching for answers as to why women hurt each other when everything is already designed to kill us.

After fourteen years to 'consider you, ponder, study, be haunted by you, love you, wonder over you, avoid you, and find no rest from you', Sylvia Likens remains unknowable. 'Sylvia wanted something from life', offered Gertrude Baniszewski upon her arrest, 'but I could not find out what it was'.[19]

1. Diana Budds, 'The Fantasy Furniture of a Feminist Icon', *Curbed*, 20 January 2022, accessed September 2023, https://www.curbed.com/2022/01/kate-millett-fantasy-furniture-sculpture-salon-94-design.html.
2. Laura Cottingham quoted in *Kate Millett, Sculptor: The First 38 Years*, ed. Kathy O'Dell, Fine Arts Gallery, University of Maryland, Baltimore, 1997, p. 22.
3. Kate Millett, 'From the Basement to the Madhouse', Kate Millett, Sculptor: The First 38 Years, Fine Arts Gallery, University of Maryland Baltimore County, 1997, p. 41.
4. Kate Millett, *The Basement: Meditations on a Human Sacrifice*. Simon & Schuster, New York, 1979, p. 11,
5. Ibid., p. 70.
6. Kate Millett, reading from The Basement at the San Francisco International Poetry Festival, 5 November 1978, *Pacifica Radio Archives*, accessed September 2023, https://archive.org/details/pacifica_radio_archives-AZ1145.
7. Lillie Gross, *Daily Record*, New Jersey, 9 September 1979, p 9.
8. Kate Millett, *The Basement*, p. 11.
9. Ibid., p. 51.
10. Youthful viciousness is nothing new; even among girls there are easily-summoned examples like 11-year-old Mary Bell who recruited a female classmate to help her strangle two boys in 1968; the torture and murder of 12-year-old Shanda Sharer by four girls in 1992; the six teenage girls who bullied and beat 14-year-old Reena Virk to death in 1997; and perhaps most relevant here for its relationship to cyclical, systematic abuse and poverty, the Mexican sisters known as 'Las Poquianchis', who abducted girls to force them into prostitution at their brothel from 1950-1964, where the bodies of at least eighty women were found on the property. Their prisoners resorted to violence against each other and even after their captors' arrest many returned to prostitution.
11. Kate Millett, *The Basement*, p. 248.
12. Kate Millett, *The Basement*, p. 111.
13. Kate Millett, reading from *The Basement*, https://archive.org/details/pacifica_radio_archives-AZ1145.
14. Kate Millett, *The Basement*, p. 62.
15. Kate Millett, *The Basement*, p. 292.
16. Virginia Kirkus, 'The Basement: Meditations on a Human Sacrifice', *Kirkus Reviews*, 1 August 1979.
17. Kathleen Barry, 'The Basement: Meditations on a Human Sacrifice' *New Women's Times Feminist Review*, issue 1, 29 February—13 March 1980, p. 6.
18. Juana Maria Paz, *Big Apple Dyke News*, issue 10, December 1982.
19. Kate Millett, *The Basement*, p. 11.

Last Night was Lucy's Birthday

Alison Peirse

Lucy and Naimie

Last night it was Lucy's birthday. We've been friends since secondary school, where we bonded over being the only girls in high school who chose thrashy guitar music and Doc Marten boots over banging techno and platform heels. I've not actually met her face to face in about eighteen months now: the pandemic has put paid to that. Lucy's husband has set up a Zoom party and, as I log in, I see Lucy, covered in sequins and inhaling prosecco as fast as she can, in internal cataclysmic horror at how old she had become. Our friend Naimie is online too, settling down to her tea at a very sophisticated 8.15pm. Despite my screen fatigue, I can't help but smile at seeing their faces.

Given that I have a PhD in horror film, the subject of *Host* (2020), the horror film that makes all Zoom chats seem queasy and tremulous, soon comes up. *Host* is about six friends who conduct a Zoom séance. The film was shot during the first lockdown, and all the actors – five female, one male – were already friends, and worked on a semi-improvised basis, from a ten-page outline. Naimie leans into her camera, smiling, and murmurs, 'but is it really *that* scary, Ally?' I suggest it is scary but lots of fun, and then am promptly dismissed by Lucy who points out my tolerance for fear is not the same as most people.

Lucy has a point. But it isn't the scariness of *Host* that makes it so strong, for me at least. *Host* is, in fact, the most real depiction of female friendship, interaction and just general girlfriend *being*, that I've ever seen in a horror film. This verisimilitude is embedded in a million tiny touches of the everyday that permeate the film. Emma – the blonde friend, with rough bunches of pigtails – has serious dark roots. Jemma's bare skin shows faint blemishes. Radina has touches of dark shadow under her eyes. When the friends think the séance is over, two-thirds of the way into the film, Caroline moans, 'ugh, I'm really sweaty' and fans her armpits. This is how good friends dress for each other, this is how you act with each other when you are truly comfortable. You can be in your pyjamas and hoodie, hair scraped off your face, because you are free to be yourself.

Lucy's birthday party concludes. I shut my laptop, and lean back, re-moulding with the sofa. I have Zoom drain, and I'm glad the party has finished, but now, the room is quiet.

It's just me and Paul, my husband, again.

Emma

I've known Emma since 2007. I submitted my PhD one Tuesday in October that year, and on the Wednesday started temping full time in administration at Leeds Beckett University. Emma was my office buddy, and on the first day we had a long discussion about the merits of the South Korean horror film *A Tale of Two Sisters* (2003), then Emma demanded that I watch *The Happiness of the Katakuris* (2001). A month later, we sat down together at the Hyde Park Picture House to watch Sion Sono's ridiculous/amazing *Exte: Hair Extensions* (2007), screened as part of Leeds International Film Festival. As we groaned in unison at the hair-pulled-out-of-the-eye-sockets-scene, I realised I had made my first horror friend.

A year later and Emma is thoroughly ensconced in my life. We decide to go see *An American Werewolf in London* (1981) at the National Media and Science Museum in Bradford. Before the screening, Emma, my brother Chris, Paul and I all knock back an inadvisable amount of beer in The Exchange pub on Market Street, then stagger over to the sold-out screening with rucksacks full of booze. We wrinkle our foreheads in united concentration as we make sure we only open our illicit cans during the noisy bits. But Chris mistimes, badly. The unmistakable fizz of Carlsberg permeates the theatre during a moment of near silence. Everyone looks. Everyone. Emma and I slink low in our seats, silent-crying-laughing. I love watching the film half-cut, with friends and family. Afterwards, I watch my excellent colleague stagger off into the sunset for her train, basking in the happy glow of communal werewolf watching.

Zosia and Helen

We're driving to Bradford Cineworld to see the 30th anniversary restoration of *Bram Stoker's Dracula* (1994), when I ask Zosia, 'this is the totally homoerotic one with Tom Cruise and Brad Pitt, isn't it?' Zosia stares at me, and Helen shouts back from the steering wheel, 'you're having us on, right?' It seems I was the only one expecting to watch a tiny Kirsten Dunst vampire for the next two hours.

Afterwards, we walk back to the car park, our faces lit up by the neon green and red lights of the Hollywood Bowl next door. We are all quiet; the neo-baroque, hyperbolic, colour-sound-costume excess of the *Apocalypse Now* of vampire films has flattened our senses. When the silence starts to worry me, I ask Zosia what she thought to the film. 'I'm still processing it', she replies slowly, and I try to help, saying, 'it's kind of like eating a really rich meal and you need time to digest it'. 'Yep', concurs Helen, as she presses the unlock button on her car keys, 'like a steak and kidney pie'. Then she adds, helpfully, 'or a plate of offal', and we all pile in the car and smile.

Amy

We are on step one of the Tories' British Roadmap out of Lockdown. Limited and necessary travel within the UK is allowed, as are outdoor gatherings of up to six people. Amy, a fellow Yorkshirewoman, now exiled in Scotland for work and love, comes down to care for her nephew and niece. I usually manage to see Amy at least a couple of times a year for horror film slumber parties at my house – although I am not allowed to pick our films anymore. For the previous two sessions, I picked *Aterrados* (English: *Terrified)* (2017) and *In Fabric* (2018), both of which have amazing first acts and then totally bomb for the rest of their duration. At that point, Amy had turned round to me and solemnly informed me that she was choosing the film next time. But our next time turned out to be sitting on a patch of grass at Roberts Park in Saltaire, two metres apart, in the punishingly cold spring sunlight, attempting to resume our acquaintance.

Not that the resumption is hard, it's like we hadn't been separated, but what was hard was how we had to resume: publicly, freezing, without a horror film to devour. What we really want is to be in elasticated waist pants, gobbling takeaway pizza, covered in seventy-five million blankets and cats, and to be thoroughly terrified, together

During the pandemic, I've managed to maintain some semblance of relationship with Zosia and Helen, who live in my village, but it is those other friendships that I enjoy with Amy, Emma, Lucy and Naimie that have temporarily evaporated. I feel their loss keenly. I don't just miss watching films at the cinema. I miss watching horror films with my girlfriends. I miss the sense of belonging this act engenders. When David in *The Lost Boys* (1987) chants, 'come join us Michael', I know exactly how Michael feels.

Me, Alone
I'm jetlagged off a flight from Boston for Ax Wound Film Festival when I realise I have to watch and write about *Talk to Me* (2022) today, right now, for a deadline. Everyone is at work, so I'm watching solo, but nonetheless, I am excited: in the past two weeks, I've watched *The Hands of Orlac* (1924) and *The Witch's Mirror* (1962) and I'm hoping that *Talk to Me* will create my ultimate triple bill of evil hand films. The joy starts early, promisingly, as Mia and Riley sing their hearts out in the car, united, but I soon realise that this is not a gang film when Mia turns up at a party and everyone ignores her. No-one wants to speak to her, she is 'clingy', 'weird', 'fucking depressing', her best friend Jade is berated for inviting her. Even when Mia grips the hand, the assembled teenagers are cruel, laughing at her not with her; Mia is their entertainment not their friend. Grief, rejection and betrayal follow demonic possession, but the primary emotion of this film is not horror. It is sadness. It is a study in solitude, an unflinching depiction of the pain of being on the outside looking in, of just begging, desperate for someone to reach out to you and whisper, 'talk to me'.

Afterwards, I'm left feeling melancholy, all alone on the sofa. I wish that Mia had had a chance to find her place amongst people who love her for who she is. I then think about what kinds of horror films make me happy and realise that I am drawn to films about gangs of friends, about groups of teens, families, siblings, the ride or die relationships where you put your life on the line, in an instant, for the ones you love. But, even more than that, I realise that, for me, the best horror film is communal, both on-screen *and* off.

When I watch a horror film with my friends, it is a gift. I get to spend an hour or two in a story where women fight back constantly, where (hopefully supernatural) evil can (sometimes) be overcome by the time the credits roll, and I get to do this in the company of the best, funniest and smartest women I know. This heady combination of screen and setting creates a world in which, as women, we are excited, we are exhilarated, and we are free.

List of works

Naomi Blacklock
Breath Hovering Beneath the Base
2016-23
sound installation, soil, PA speaker, fabric, rope, granite stones, 15:19 mins (looped). Fabric tent construction thanks to: Elisabeth Soo. Courtesy the artist.

Mia Boe
A Desolate Primitive Place 2023
lightbox, digital print, synthetic polymer paint, 80.0 x 100.0 cm.
Courtesy the artist and Sutton Gallery, Melbourne.

I Suspect 2023
lightbox, digital print, synthetic polymer paint, 80.0 x 100.0 cm.
Courtesy the artist and Sutton Gallery, Melbourne.

Louise Bourgeois
Spider 1995
drypoint on paper, 54.0 x 40.3 cm.
© The Easton Foundation. Licensed by Copyright Agency, Sydney. Photo: Christopher Burke.

Arched Figure 1993
drypoint on paper, 39.7 x 55.9 cm.
© The Easton Foundation. Licensed by Copyright Agency, Sydney. Photo: Christopher Burke.

Untitled (*Safety Pins)* 1991
drypoint on paper, 49.4 x 56.0 cm.
© The Easton Foundation. Licensed by Copyright Agency, Sydney. Photo: Christopher Burke.

Cybele Cox
The Hag 2023
oil and gesso on ceramic, 50.0 x 115.0 x 90.0 cm.
Courtesy the artist and Yavuz Gallery, Sydney.

Goat Head 2017
oil and gesso on ceramic, 60.0 x 60.0 x 20.0 cm.
Courtesy the artist and Yavuz Gallery, Sydney.

Karla Dickens
Warrior Woman XIV 2017
mixed media, 30.0 x 18.0 x 10.0 cm.
Courtesy the artist and STATION, Sydney.

Warrior Woman VI 2017
mixed media, 30.0 x 18.0 x 10.0 cm.
Courtesy the artist and STATION, Sydney.

Warrior Woman IV 2017
mixed media, 30.0 x 18.0 x 10.0 cm.
Courtesy the artist and STATION, Sydney.

Lonnie Hutchinson
Equality 2016
ink and acrylic on rag paper, 50.0 x 35.0 cm.
Courtesy the artist and Jonathan Smart Gallery, Christchurch.

Justice 2016
ink and acrylic on rag paper, 50.0 x 35.0 cm.
Courtesy the artist and Jonathan Smart Gallery, Christchurch.

Freedom 2016
ink and acrylic on rag paper, 50.0 x 35.0 cm.
Courtesy the artist and Jonathan Smart Gallery, Christchurch.

Naomi Kantjuriny
Mamu (Good Spirits) 2023
ink on paper, 76.0 x 56.5 cm (each).
Courtesy the artist and Tjala Arts, Amata.

Minyoung Kim
Staring 2021
pencil and oil pastel on paper, 29.7 x 21.0 cm.
Courtesy the artist.

The Bath 2021
pencil on paper, 21.0 x 29.7 cm.
Courtesy the artist.

The Grass 2021
oil pastel on paper, 21.0 x 29.7 cm.
Courtesy the artist.

The Night 2021
acrylic on paper, 21.0 x 29.7 cm.
Courtesy the artist.

Live Drawing Books I 2018
single-channel video, 1:45 mins (looped).
Courtesy the artist.

Live Drawing Books II 2018
single-channel video, 2:01 mins (looped).
Courtesy the artist.

Live Drawing Books III 2018
single-channel video, 1:41 mins (looped).
Courtesy the artist.

Maria Kozic
Miss January 1999
synthetic polymer paint on canvas,
189.5 x 170.0 cm.
Courtesy the artist and Neon Parc,
Melbourne.

Miss February 1999
synthetic polymer paint on canvas,
123.0 x 214.0 cm.
Courtesy the artist and Neon Parc,
Melbourne.

Miss March 1999
synthetic polymer paint on canvas,
168.5 x 138.0 cm.
Courtesy the artist and Neon Parc,
Melbourne.

Miss April 1999
synthetic polymer paint on canvas,
189.0 x 107.0 cm.
Courtesy the artist and Neon Parc,
Melbourne.

Miss May 1999
synthetic polymer paint on canvas.
168.5 x 138.0 cm.
Courtesy the artist and Neon Parc,
Melbourne.

Miss June 1999
synthetic polymer paint on canvas,
183.5 x 152.5 cm.
Courtesy the artist and Neon Parc,
Melbourne.

Miss July 1999
synthetic polymer paint on canvas,
168.0 x 138.0 cm.
Courtesy the artist and Neon Parc,
Melbourne.

Miss August 1999
synthetic polymer paint on canvas,
138.0 x 214.0 cm.
Courtesy the artist and Neon Parc,
Melbourne.

Miss September 1999
synthetic polymer paint on canvas,
123.0 x 214.0 cm.
Courtesy the artist and Neon Parc,
Melbourne.

Miss October 1999
synthetic polymer paint on canvas,
189.0 x 138.0 cm.
Courtesy the artist and Neon Parc,
Melbourne.

Miss November 1999
synthetic polymer paint on canvas,
198.5 x 132.0 cm.
Courtesy the artist and Neon Parc,
Melbourne.

Miss December 1999
synthetic polymer paint on canvas,
123.0 x 214.0 cm.
Courtesy the artist and Neon Parc,
Melbourne.

Jemima Lucas
Stifled forces - Constantly Swelling. Will the Levee break? 2023
punctured plaster wall, mild steel forged and beaten anchor, stainless steel cable, mangled steel reinforcement, bronze ox tongue, stainless steel wire cable, stainless steel turnbuckles, structural eye bolt, dimensions variable.
Courtesy the artist.

Clare Milledge
Badb: bro im glitched 2023
oil on toughened glass, reclaimed timber frame (Agathis robusta), 120.0 x 120.0 cm.
Courtesy the artist and STATION, Sydney.

Tracey Moffatt
A Haunting 2021–2023
single-channel video, 1:37 mins (looped).
Courtesy the artist and Roslyn Oxley9 Gallery, Sydney.

Theron Debris
Fortuna 2023
digital print, 100.0 x 60.0 cm.
Courtesy the artist.

Bottom Feeder 2023
digital print, 100.0 x 60.0 cm.
Courtesy the artist.

Sweet Tooth 2023
digital print, 100.0 x 60.0 cm.
Courtesy the artist.

Dolorosa 2023
digital print, 100.0 x 60.0 cm.
Courtesy the artist.

Painted Love 2023
digital print, 100.0 x 60.0 cm.
Courtesy the artist.

Vile Jelly 2023
digital print, 100.0 x 60.0 cm.
Courtesy the artist.

Amniotic 2023
digital print, 100.0 x 60.0 cm.
Courtesy the artist.

Chuparrosa 2023
digital print, 100.0 x 60.0 cm.
Courtesy the artist.

Suzan Pitt
Visitation 2011
single-channel video, 8:00 mins.
Courtesy the artist and the Suzan Pitt Estate.

Julia Robinson
Double Stumps 2021
scythe, linen, thread, steel, pewter, fixings, 140.0 x 150.0 x 20.0 cm.
Courtesy the artist and Hugo Michell Gallery, Adelaide.

The Pledge 2021-22
linen, thread, scythe handles, steel, tacks, fixings, 160.0 x 155.0 x 25.0 cm.
Courtesy the artist and Hugo Michell Gallery, Adelaide.

Burrow Mump 2022
linen, thread, scythe handle, blade, steel, 110.0 x 130.0 x 25.0 cm. Courtesy the artist and Hugo Michell Gallery, Adelaide.

Tatterdemalion 2022
linen, thread, found embroidery, scythe, steel, 155.0 x 75.0 x 30.0 cm.
Courtesy the artist and Hugo Michell Gallery, Adelaide.

Marianna Simnett
The Udder 2014
single-channel HD video with sound, 15:30 mins (looped).
Courtesy the artist and Société, Berlin.

Heather B Swann
Never let me go 2023
starched linen, wire, brass, vintage wooden hair roller sticks, 500 sets of linen eyelashes, dimensions variable, thanks to: Charlotte Minnett and Susan Jones. Courtesy the artist and STATION, Melbourne.

The Three Sisters 2023
wood, forged steel, ink, stain, lacquer, wax, paper, binder, modelling stuff, pigment, marble dust, glass, 240.0 x 275.0 x 60.0 cm, thanks to: Les Guilfoyle The Flying Anvil, Dylan Black Furniture, Stuart Houghton and Ole Windfeld Petersen. Courtesy the artist and STATION, Melbourne.

Human Frailty 2023
wood, glass, modelling stuff, aquamarine, ruby, garnet, forged steel, lacquer, brass
13 elements, 11.7 x 6.8 x 3.5 cm (each) plus bracket, thanks to: Timothy Smullen Formspace.
Courtesy the artist and STATION, Melbourne.

Kellie Wells
Through Catherine 2019
framed C-Type photograph, 113.0 x 190.0 cm.
Courtesy the artist.

Skeleton Key 2020-2022
hand built glazed ceramic skulls and roses on brass rings and rod, 140.0 x 40.0 cm.
Courtesy the artist.

Through Lilith 2023
hand-built glazed ceramic skull beads, grown crystals on human and synthetic hair on brass rings and brass rods, dimensions variable.
Courtesy the artist.

Through Louise 2023
hand-built glazed ceramic skull beads, grown crystals on human and synthetic hair on brass rings and brass rods, dimensions variable.
Courtesy the artist.

Through Leonora 2023
hand-built glazed ceramic skull beads, grown crystals on human and synthetic hair on brass rings and brass rods, dimensions variable.
Courtesy the artist.

Through Morrigan 2023
hand-built glazed ceramic skull beads, grown crystals on human and synthetic hair on brass rings and brass rods, dimensions variable.
Courtesy the artist.

Through Lucifer 2023
hand-built glazed ceramic skull beads, grown crystals on human and synthetic hair on brass rings and brass rods, dimensions variable.
Courtesy the artist.

Zamara Zamara
Like Pulling Teeth 2023
glazed stoneware, steel, dimensions variable.
Courtesy the artist.

Ceramic Gestures 2019-2023
glazed stoneware, dimensions variable.
Courtesy the artist.

Naomi Blacklock

born 1990, Alice Springs
lives and works in Meanjin/Brisbane, Australia

Naomi Blacklock's practice maps the nexus of embodied performance, cultural heritage and gender identity. Working across a range of media, from experimental sound and video installation to performance and sculpture, her work creatively examines the mythologies, archetypes and harmful histories of gender and cultural identity through an intersectional feminist lens. Her ritualised sound objects and performances are intended to amplify the body and the voice through performative corporeal precision and aural screaming.

In 2019 Naomi was awarded her PhD from Queensland University of Technology for her thesis *Conjuring Alterity: Refiguring the Witch and The Female Scream in Contemporary Art*. Her work has been presented at Hobart's Art Festival, Dark Mofo and in numerous galleries and artist-run Initiatives both locally and nationally. With broad experience in the visual arts sector, Naomi is a current board member of Metro Arts, has served as the Director of Boxcopy Contemporary Art Space, and is a Founding Co-Director of Clutch Collective ARI.

Mia Boe

born 1997, Meanjin/Brisbane
lives and works in Naarm/Melbourne, Australia

Mia Boe is a painter with Butchulla and Burmese ancestry. The inheritance and disinheritance of both cultures is the focus of her practice. Boe's paintings respond, sometimes obliquely, to historical and contemporary acts of violence perpetrated on the people and lands of Burma and Australia.

Boe received a Bachelor of Art, majoring in Art History, from the University of Queensland in 2020. In 2021, she was a recipient of the Brett Whiteley Travelling Scholarship and is a current studio artist at Gertrude Contemporary. Recent solo exhibitions include *Going Insein,* Gertrude Contemporary Glasshouse, Melbourne, 2023; *Suspicion is proof enough*, Sutton Gallery, Melbourne, 2023; *The Trial,* Sydney Contemporary with Black Art Projects, Sydney 2022; *Futures Lost,* Penny Contemporary, Hobart 2022; *K'gari means paradise in Butchulla,* CARPARK, Milani Gallery, Sydney 2021; and *Black Devil,* Open House Collective with Blaklash Projects, Brisbane, 2021.

Recent group exhibitions include *Thin Skin,* Monash University Museum of Art, Melbourne, 2023; *Melbourne Now*, National Gallery of Victoria, Melbourne, 2023; *While You Were Sleeping Volume 2*, Ambush Gallery, Canberra, 2022; *Portrait 23: Identity*, National Portrait Gallery, Canberra, 2022; *Dingo Project,* Hervey Bay Regional Gallery, Queensland, 2022; and *Making Place: 100 Views of Brisbane,* Museum of Brisbane, Brisbane, 2022.

Louise Bourgeois
born 1911, Paris
died 2010, New York, USA

Louise Bourgeois was a French-American artist born in Paris in 1911. A prolific artist, her work explored themes related to family, sexuality, the body, death and the unconscious, particularly as they connected to childhood, psychoanalysis and therapy.

In the mid- to late-1930s, she studied at the École des beaux-arts in Paris before moving to New York in 1938. Throughout her life, she exhibited widely in the United States and Europe, including major solo and group exhibitions at the Museum of Modern Art, New York, 1982-83; Documenta 9, Kassel, Germany, 1992; 45th La Biennale di Venezia, Venice, 1993; the São Paulo Biennial, São Paulo, 1996; Guggenheim Museum, Bilbao, 2001-02; State Hermitage Museum, St Petersburg, 2001-03; and Tate Modern, London, 2007-08 – an exhibition that travelled to the Guggenheim Museum, 2008.

Bourgeois' achievements have been recognised with a fellowship from the National Endowment for the Arts, 1973, membership in the American Academy of Arts and Sciences, 1981, a grand prize in sculpture from the French Ministry of Culture, 1991, the National Medal of Arts, 1997, the Leone d'Oro, 1999, a Medal of Honour from the Pennsylvania Academy of Fine Arts in Philadelphia, 2005, the 2006 Intrepid Award from the National Organization for Women, 2006, and the Woman Award from the United Nations and Women Together, 2007, among others.

Cybele Cox
born 1971, Gadigal Country/Sydney
lives and works Guringai Country/Avalon, Australia

Cybele Cox's practice explores representations of women in the Western art canon, blending motifs drawn from ancient feminine symbols, occult mysticism, classicism and fashion. Using hand built ceramic totems and figures, painting, drawing and costume, Cox hybridises human and animal forms, fusing symbols from the mythic world with utopian fantasies. In doing so, she attempts to reconstruct a new belief system from remnants of old ones, discarding the broken, hegemonic narratives and elevating those which were previously underestimated or hidden. For Cox, her works function as a means of entry into imagining an alternative version of events. They invite viewers to unstick and unstack themselves, and then rebuild piece by piece, in a call for a re-flowering of the spiritual, and ultimately, a new feminist order.

Cox holds a Master of Fine Art from the Sydney College of Art, and a Bachelor of Fine Art from the University of New South Wales. Her work has been included in curated exhibitions across Australia including *Once More With Feeling*, Ngununggula Regional Gallery, Bowral, 2023; *The Stand Ups*, Bus Projects, Melbourne, 2022; *Nothing Human is Alien to Me*, Ideas Platform, Artspace, Sydney, 2019; *Romance Died Romantically*, Strange Neighbour, Melbourne, 2015; and the 2022 Australian Ceramics Triennale.

Theron Debris
born 1986, Gadigal Country/Sydney
lives and works in New York, USA

Theron Debris is a cross-displinary artist and ritualist. His practice is underpinned by a deep preoccupation with occult philosophy, folklore, ritual and ceremony, and the religious practices of the subaltern - an ongoing enquiry grounded in his Indigenous (Wiraduri/Ngyiampaa-Wailwan) and trans identities.

In one of his other lives, Debris has produced a prolific body of work as the multi-hyphenate artist, author and curator SJ Norman, whose twenty-year career embraced a wide variety of disciplines, including long-durational performance, sculpture, social practice, sound, film and literature. His recent exhibition and acquisition history as SJ Norman includes the National Gallery of Australia, Biennale of Sydney, and National Indigenous Art Triennial. He is the recipient of numerous major awards for art, including the 67th Blake Prize, 2022. A distinguished writer, his first book - the uncanny fiction collection *Permafrost* published in 2021 by UQP - was nominated for seven major literary prizes in Australia, including the Stella Prize, 2022 and the Australian Society for Literature Gold medal, 2022. His work has been featured in Artforum, New York Times and Vogue, among others.

SJ Norman and Theron Debris continue to occupy one body as distinct creative forces: while Norman continues to work as an artist, author and curator, Debris's visual practice is focused on photographic abstraction, illustration, garment and textile design. His work utilises an idiosyncratic process of distorting found images, layering digital, analogue and painterly processes to produce an exuberant array of speculative forms. Where Norman's work is known for its formal and aesthetic austerity, Debris's work is playful, hyperchromatic, wilfully trashy and embraces a gamut of aesthetic influences.

Karla Dickens
born 1967, Gadigal Country/Sydney
lives and works Bundjalung Country/Lismore, Australia

Karla Dickens is an artist of Wiradjuri, Irish and German heritage. Through her multidisciplinary practice – spanning painting, photography, video, collage, sculpture and installation – Dickens brings a black humour to her unflinching interrogation of subjects such as race, gender and injustice. Described as a 'found-object' virtuoso, her practice often places overlooked or discarded objects into new contexts to interrogate Australian culture, contest histories and agitate for change.

Dickens graduated from the National Art School, Sydney, with a Diploma of Fine Arts in 1993 and a Bachelor of Fine Arts in 2000..

Recent exhibitions include *NIRIN: 22nd Biennale of Sydney*, Sydney, 2020; *Know My Name: Australian Women Artists 1900 to Now,* National Gallery of Australia, Canberra, 2020; *Monster Theatres: Adelaide Biennial of Australian Art*, Art Gallery of South Australia, Adelaide, 2020; *Defying Empire: 3rd National Indigenous Art Triennial, National Gallery of Australia, Canberra*, 2017; and *The National 2017: New Australian Art*, Carriageworks, Sydney, 2017. In 2023 Dickens' major survey exhibition *Embracing Shadows* opened at Campbelltown Arts Centre, spanning thirty years of practice. Dickens' work is held in major collections including the National Gallery of Australia, National Portrait Gallery, Art Gallery of New South Wales, Art Gallery of South Australia, Art Gallery of Western Australia, National Gallery of Victoria, and the Museum of Contemporary Art, among others.

Lonnie Hutchinson
born 1963, Tāmaki Makaurau/Auckland
lives and works Ōtautahi/Christchurch, Aotearoa/New Zealand

Lonnie Hutchinson (Ngāti kuri ki Ngāi Tahu, Samoan, Celtic) is a multi-disciplinary artist whose practice comments astutely on aspects of indigeneity in the contemporary world.

Hutchinson's signature cut-out work extend across a range of materials, including black builder's paper, vintage wallpapers, acrylic, steel and aluminium. Fusing the personal and political, she uses various motifs that reference her cultural heritage to comment on ancient traditions and the effects of colonisation.

Public commissions include *Hana*, Te Pae Christchurch Convention Centre, 2022; *Aroha ki te Ora*, 2020, perforated and folded aluminium panels that tell the Ngāi Tahu creation story, Britomart, Auckland; *Pikihuia i te ao, i te pō*, and *Kahu Matarau*, 2017, two large scale integrations into the exterior of the Christchurch Justice and Emergency Services Precinct; *Aroha Atu, Aroha Mai*, 2015, a neon art work in Manukau City; *Te Waharoa ki te ao Mārama*, 2012, Hamilton Lake; and *Honoa ki te Hono Tawhiti*, 2011, Auckland Art Gallery. Hutchinson's work can be found in the the collections of the Auckland Art Gallery Toi o Tamaki; Christchurch Art Gallery Te Puna o Waiwhetu; the Hocken Library, Dunedin; Queensland Art Gallery; National Gallery of Australia; The Chartwell Collection; and in private collections in New Zealand and abroad.

Hutchinson is represented by The Central Art Gallery in Ōtautahi Christchurch, and Milford Galleries in Ōtepoti Dunedin.

Naomi Kantjuriny
born 1944, Victory Downs
lives and works Anangu Pitjantjatjara Yankunytjatjara Lands, Australia

Naomi Kantjuriny (Pitjantjatjara) is a prolific painter who has been working at Tjala Arts since 2001. An excellent hunter, basket maker and wood carver, Kantjuriny has become renowned for her unique works in ink on paper. Recognised for her knowledge of the Tjukurpa stories of her Country, Kantjuriny is also a *Ngangkari*, a traditional healer through treatments and practices of the mind, body and spirit. Kantjuriny paints the Mamu, which are mainly harmful, dangerous spirit forces, which come in different forms such as evil spirits, monsters, and illness, with varying powers. Kantjuriny is trained to release the Mamu from sick people and to help people find their spirit taken by the Mamu.

Kantjuriny is one third of the Mitakiki Women's Collaborative alongside artists Mona Mitakiki and Tjimpayi Presley. Together they paint kapi tjukurla (rock holes) that relate to the Kungkarangkalpa tjukurpa. Her collaborative and solo work has exhibited nationally including was shortlisted for the Telstra Work on Paper Award at the 2023 National Aboriginal Torres Strait Islander Art Awards.

Her work is included in public and private collections across Australia including the Art Gallery of South Australia, Adelaide and the Art Gallery of NSW, Sydney.

Minyoung Kim
born 1989, Seoul
lives and works London, UK

Minyoung Kim's work mirrors her innermost feelings, ones that language fails to express. By using unstretched raw canvas, she portrays, in a soft manner, ironic scenes that combine what she refers to as strange but cute elements. It's in this ambivalence, both light and serious, that she explores and reveals her inner self.

Kim graduated from Sungshin Women's University, Seoul, with a Bachelor in Painting in 2014. Kim currently resides in London where she completed her Master of Fine Art at the Slade School of Fine Art in 2021.

Kim's solo exhibition *Night Fever* was the inaugural exhibition in Taymour Grahne Projects' The Artist Room gallery, London, 2023. Previous solo exhibitions were held at Aout Gallery, Beirut, 2021; Place Mak, Seoul, 2016; Seogyo Art Space, Seoul, 2016; among others.

Recent group exhibitions were held at the National Taiwan Arts Education Centre, Taipei; Artime Art Centre, China, and Fortnight Institute, New York.

Maria Kozic
born 1957, Naarm/Melbourne
lives and works in New York, USA

Maria Kozic works across painting, sculpture, photography and film. Through the lens of gender and feminist politics, she is known for engaging with cult cinema, music, popular culture, advertising and DIY punk aesthetics. Kozic's practice has often drawn on the depictions and tropes of women, monsters and creatures in horror and exploitation films.

Solo exhibitions include *Wonderland*, Neon Parc, Melbourne, 2022; *Welcome to my Nightmeera,* Posteritati Gallery, New York, 2014; *Collide-O-Rama,* Hazlehurst Regional Gallery, New South Wales, 2009; *MK Paintings,* Wallspace, New York, 1999; *Birth of Blue Boy,* Museum of Contemporary Art, Sydney, 1992; and *Maria Kozic,* Institute of Modern Art, Brisbane, 1988.

Group exhibitions include *Unfinished Business: Perspectives on art and feminism,* Australian Centre for Contemporary Art, Melbourne, 2017-2018; *Pop to Popism*, Art Gallery of New South Wales, Sydney, 2014; *Mixed Tape 1980s: Appropriation, Subculture, Critical Style,* National Gallery of Victoria, Melbourne, 2013; *Gift Shop. Another Year In LA,* Los Angeles, California 2007*; Objects*, Printed Matter New York, 1998; *Perspecta '95,* Art Gallery of New South Wales, Sydney, 1995; and *Aperto, Venice Biennale*, Venice,1986.

Kozic's work is held in public collections including National Gallery of Australia; National Gallery of Victoria; Art Gallery of New South Wales; and Art Gallery of Western Australia; and in private collections in Australia, United States, England and Japan.

Jemima Lucas
born 1995, Naarm/Melbourne
lives and works Naarm/Melbourne, Australia

Jemima Lucas is a multi-disciplinary artist whose practice intersects conceptual and spatial modalities of research, contemporary sculpture, assemblage and performance. Her work penetrates and dilates discourses around relativity, autonomy and material/immaterial bodies. With materials enacting the primary point of departure in her practice, Lucas extends an acknowledgement of the First Nations people on the lands from which they are sourced.

Lucas has presented solo and duo exhibitions nationally including Sawtooth ARI, Launceston, 2023; Produce Gallery, Melbourne, 2023; Incinerator Gallery, Melbourne, 2022, and Feltspace, Adelaide, 2021. She has also been curated into group exhibitions including Airspace, Sydney, 2023; Stanley Street Gallery, Sydney, 2022; Tsukuba University, Tokyo, 2022; and Monash Prato Fine Art, Prato, 2017.

Lucas completed a Bachelor of Fine Arts at Monash University in 2019, before undertaking an Honours of Fine Art at VCA in 2021.

Clare Milledge
born 1977, Gadigal Country/Sydney
lives and works Gadigal Country/Sydney, Australia

Dr. Clare Milledge is an artist and academic who explores the artist-shaman archetype to connect with contemporary ecologies and existence. Employing enigmatic historical frameworks, she explores how magic and the occult can be used to re-evaluate westernised connections to non-human entities, including animals, nature and language.

Guided by intuition and grounded in fieldwork, Milledge gathers material from a diverse range of sources including conversations, poems, folklore, literature, the occult, political ecology, feminist theory, MMORPG chat rooms, Tinder profiles, and garden walks. These eclectic elements coalesce to form public assemblage, where her iconic hinterglasmalerei paintings serve as keystones. This technique, employed by Byzantine painters, entails the application of oil paint on the reverse side of glass.

Milledge's work has been included in significant exhibitions including *rīvus: 23rd Biennale of Sydney*, 2022; *NGV Triennial,* National Gallery of Victoria, Melbourne, 2020; and *Magic Object*, Adelaide Biennial of Australian Art, Art Gallery of South Australia, 2016. Her work has been shown at institutions including Buxton Contemporary; University of Queensland Art Museum; Perth Institute of Contemporary Art, and Artspace, Sydney. Her work is held in significant public and private collections including National Gallery of Victoria, University of Melbourne, Monash University Collection, and Artbank.

Milledge holds a Doctor of Philosophy from Sydney College of the Arts, the University of Sydney, 2013, and completed her Honours year at the Statenskunst Akademi, Oslo, 2006.

Tracey Moffatt
born 1977, Meanjin/Brisbane,
lives and works Gadigal Country/Sydney, Australia

Tracey Moffatt is one of Australia's most renowned contemporary artists. Working predominantly in photography and film for over three decades, Moffatt is known as a powerful visual storyteller whose narratives are often self-referential and implied, exploring her own childhood memories, and broader issues of race, gender, sexuality and identity.

Moffatt has held over one hundred solo exhibitions in Europe, the United States and Australia. Her films, including *Nightcries – A Rural Tragedy*, 1989, and *Bedevil*, 1993, have been screened at the Cannes Film Festival, the Dia Centre for the Arts in New York, and the National Centre for Photography in Paris.

Moffatt presented Australia at the 57th Venice Biennale, 2017, with her solo exhibition *MY HORIZON* in the Australian Pavilion. Moffatt has exhibited in numerous national and international art exhibitions and film festivals over three decades. In 2012, a retrospective program of her films was held at the Museum of Modern Art, New York. Moffatt first gained significant critical acclaim when her short film, *Night Cries*, was selected for official competition at the 1990 Cannes Film Festival. Her first feature film, *beDevil*, was also selected for Cannes in 1993. She held a major exhibition at the Dia Center for the Arts in New York in 1997-98, and in 2003, a large retrospective exhibition of her work was held at the Museum of Contemporary Art, Sydney, which also travelled to the Hasselblad Museum in Sweden.

Suzan Pitt
born 1943, Missouri
died 2019, New Mexico, USA

Suzan Pitt was an American experimental film animator and painter whose surreal, psychological and idiosyncratic works create interior worlds that draw upon themes of sexuality, mortality and unconsciousness.

Pitt has presented individual exhibitions include The Ginza Art Space, Tokyo; Whitney American Museum of Art, New York; Holly Solomon Gallery, New York; Cantor-Lemberg Gallery, Detroit; Hans Mayer Gallery, Dusseldorf; and the Delahunty Gallery, New York; among others.

Her film *Asparagus* 1979 premiered at the Whitney Museum in the same year and ran for two years with David Lynch's *Eraserhead* in the midnight shows at the Waverly Theater and the NuArt Theater in Los Angeles. A retrospective of Suzan Pitt's prize-winning animated films was presented at the Museum of Modern Art, New York, in 2017.

Pitt's paintings and films are held in collections at the Walker Art Center, Minneapolis; Museum of Modern Art, New York; Stedeliik Museum Amsterdam, and the Academy of Motion Picture Arts and Sciences, Los Angeles. Her animated films have been featured at hundreds of prestigious venues around the world including the Sundance Film Festival, New York Film Festival, London Film Festival, and Ottawa International Animated Film Festival.

A former Associate Professor at Harvard University, Pitt received a Guggenheim Fellowship, a Rockefeller Fellowship and three production grants from the National Endowment of the Arts.

Julia Robinson
born 1981, Kaurna Country/Adelaide
lives and works in Kaurna Country/Adelaide, Australia

Julia Robinson is a visual artist working in the fields of sculpture and installation. Looking to her British ancestry as a starting point, Robinson's work reflects an interest in folklore, pre-Christian rituals, and calendrical customs relating to the cycle of the seasons, growth and decay. She frequently employs historical costuming and sewing techniques to create artworks that sit at the intersection of folklore, ritual and folk horror, examining enduring narratives around sacrifice, sex and death.

Since graduating from Adelaide Central School of Art, Robinson has exhibited regularly and been the recipient of a number of grants and awards. Recent exhibitions include *Eerie Pageantry*, City Gallery Wellington, Wellington, 2023; *The Beckoning Blade*, Hugo Michell Gallery, Adelaide, 2022; *Monster Theatres: 2020 Adelaide Biennial of Australian Art*; The Santos Museum of Economic Botany, Adelaide, 2020; *The National: New Australian Art,* Museum of Contemporary Art, Sydney, 2019; and *Versus Rodin: Bodies across space and time*, Art Gallery of South Australia, Adelaide, 2017.

Robinson lectures in the Bachelor of Visual Arts program at Adelaide Central School of Art. Her work is held in the collections of the Art Gallery of South Australia, Museum of Contemporary Art, Artbank, Tamworth Regional Gallery, and various private collections. She is represented by Hugo Michell Gallery.

Marianna Simnett
born 1986, London
lives and works in Berlin, Germany

Marianna Simnett is a multidisciplinary visual artist who uses vivid and visceral means to explore the body as a site of transformation. In psychologically charged works that challenge both herself and the viewer, Simnett imagines radical new worlds filled with untamed thoughts, strange tales and desires.

Simnett's work has been exhibited internationally in solo exhibitions at venues including City Gallery Wellington, Wellington, 2020; Institute of Modern Art, Brisbane, 2019; Frans Hals Museum, Haarlem, 2019; Kunsthalle Zürich, Zürich, 2019; Museum für Moderne Kunst, Frankfurt, 2018; The New Museum, New York, 2018; and Zabludowicz Collection, London, 2018. Selected recent group exhibitions include *The Milk of Dreams: 59th Venice Biennale*, 2022; *Espressioni: The Epilogue*, Castello di Rivoli, Turin, 2022; Prize of the Böttcherstraße, Kunsthalle Bremen, Bremen, 2022; *British Art Show 9*, various cities, 2021; *A Fire in My Belly*, Julia Stoschek Collection, Berlin, 2021; *Unprecedented Times*, Kunsthaus Bregenz, 2020; and *The Body Electric*, Walker Art Center, Minneapolis, 2019. Her work *The Severed Tail* was recently shown at the 66th BFI London Film Festival, British Film Institute, London, 2022. She is represented by Société, Berlin.

Heather B Swann
born 1961, nipaluna/Hobart
lives and works in nipaluna/Hobart, Australia

Heather B. Swann's work embodies a dialectic of the personal and the political, the physical and the conceptual. Working from visual and bodily sensation, from intense emotion and thoughtful meditation, and employing imagery drawn from museum culture, history, mythology and natural science, Swann distils a poetry of intimacy and anguish: objects and pictures that reflect and refract her and our existential moment. While her subjects, signs and symbols are enormously varied, they present a dark beauty through an unmistakeable, idiosyncratic sensibility.

Best known for expressive figurative sculptures and gestural black ink drawings, Swann's expansive practice extends to painting, video, installation and performance. Swann has presented over twenty solo shows since 1993, including *Leda and the Swan,* Tarrawarra Museum of Art, Victoria, 2021, and *Nervous*, National Gallery of Australia, Canberra, 2016. Her work has been curated into significant group exhibitions, including *Inner Sanctum: Adelaide Biennial of Australian Art*, Art Gallery of South Australia, Adelaide, 2024; *The National 4: Australian Art Now*, Art Gallery of New South Wales, Sydney, 2023; *Setouchi Triennale*, Japan, 2022; *Know My Name: Australian Women Artists 1900 to Now*, National Gallery of Australia, Canberra, 2021.

Her work is held in various public collections, including National Gallery of Australia, Art Gallery of New South Wales, National Gallery of Victoria, Art Gallery of South Australia and Heide Museum of Modern Art.

Kellie Wells
born 1971, kanamaluka country/ Launceston
lives and works in Naarm/Melbourne, Australia

Kellie Wells is an artist, researcher and educator with over thirty years of study and practice. Her multidisciplinary and contemplative practice explores the multidimensional nature of subjectivity and lived experience within our historical entanglements with meaning, mystery, magic and matter. Her research neologism 'Auto//Mysticism' investigates and combines medieval female mystic knowledges, alchemical symbolism and coded languages, with autobiography and metaphysical notions of the self-as-subject.

Wells has presented solo and group exhibitions at Fiona Sidney Myer Gallery, University of Melbourne, Melbourne, 2023; Sawtooth ARI, Launceston, 2021; ArtSpace Mackay, Mackay, 2018; Seventh Gallery, Melbourne, 2017; Bundoora Homestead Art Centre, Melbourne, 2017; Abbotsford Convent, Melbourne, 2017; West Space, Melbourne, 2012. Her PhD project titled *The Alchemy of Auto//Mysticism: Subjectivity(s) from the In-Between* was exhibited at Fiona Sidney Myer Gallery, VCA/MCM, Melbourne, 2022.

Wells is currently tutoring for the Critical and Theoretical Studies program at the Victorian College of the Arts, University of Melbourne and maintains an ongoing commitment to her art community through a number of reading groups, mentoring, collaborative projects.

Her work has been acquired by private collectors and institutions such as the Museum of Old and New Art.

Zamara Zamara
born 1994, Naarm/Melbourne
lives and works in Naarm/Melbourne, Australia

Zamara Zamara is an antidisciplinary artist, working predominantly with ceramics, fabric and fibres, photography, metal and wooden structures; they produce reflexive sculptures, satirical imagery, and site responsive installations. Zamara's practice is informed by religion and mythologies, playing out a tongue-in-cheek indulgence in the monstrous-feminine and grotesque queerness. They investigate the fabrication of queered iconography and propaganda, with a consideration of how non-dominant histories may be located and alternate futures may be actualised.

Zamara has exhibited nationally with solo exhibitions including *made jagged* at Cool Change Contemporary, Boorloo/Perth, 2021 and *The use of most resistance* at Trocadero Art Space, Melbourne, 2019. Their work has been shown in numerous local curated exhibitions, most recently at TCB Gallery, 2023; Fiona and Sidney Myer Gallery, 2023; Blak Dot Gallery, 2022 and Bundoora Homestead Art Centre, 2021. They were the recipient of the People's Choice Award at the Incinerator Art Award in 2021, and an NGV Women's Association Award in 2018.

In 2020 Zamara was selected for a School House Studios Residency and Grant for *Worn to be Wild*, a project built around collaborative textile works with local artists.

Contributors

Jessica Balanzategui is Senior Lecturer in Media at RMIT University, Melbourne. Her widely published research examines how technological change impacts screen entertainment cultures and aesthetics, particularly horror and the Gothic, and children's media. Exploring the intersections between these two seemingly diametrically opposed genres, Balanzategui's current focus is screen genres *for* and *about* children that trouble expectations and definitions of 'child appropriateness'. Her books include *Netflix, Dark Fantastic Genres, and Intergenerational Viewing: Family Watch Together TV*, Routledge, 2023, (with Djoymi Baker and Diana Sandars); *Monstrous Beings and Media Cultures: Folk Monsters, Im/materiality, Regionality*, Amsterdam University Press, 2023, (with Allison Craven); and *The Uncanny Child in Transnational Cinema: Ghosts of Futurity at the Turn of the 21st Century*, Amsterdam University Press, 2018. Balanzategui is the Founding Editor of Amsterdam University Press's book series, *Horror and Gothic Media Cultures*.

Jessica Clark is a proud palawa/pallawah woman with English, Irish, Turkish, and French ancestry. She is an independent curator, writer and researcher with a background in art history and art education. Clark currently holds the position of Yalingwa Curator at the Australian Centre for Contemporary Art, 2022-24. Recent exhibitions include *Between Waves*, Australian Centre for Contemporary Art, Melbourne, 2023, and touring nationally, 2024-2026; *breathing space*, Margaret Lawrence Gallery, Melbourne, 2021; *In and of this place*, Benalla Art Gallery (online), 2021; *one (&) another*, Margaret Lawrence Gallery, Melbourne, 2020; and co-curation of *Experimenta Life Forms: International*

Triennial of Media Art, touring nationally, 2021-2023. She is alumni of the International Curators Program: Asia Pacific Triennial x TarraWarra Biennial, 2021-2023, PIAD First Nations Colloquium, South Africa, 2019, Wesfarmers Indigenous Arts Leadership Program, 2018, and the First Nations Curators Program, Venice Biennale, 2017. Clark holds a PhD degree from the Victorian College of the Arts, University of Melbourne.

Barbara Creed is Redmond Barry Distinguished Professor Emeritus at the University of Melbourne. She is the author of eight books, including *The Monstrous-Feminine: Film, Feminism, Psychoanalysis*, 1993; *Darwin's Screens*: *Evolutionary Aesthetics, Time & Sexual Display In The Cinema*, 2009; *Stray: Human-Animal Ethics in The Anthropocene*, 2017; and *Return of the Monstrous-Feminine: Feminist New Wave Cinema*, 2022. Her recent research is in feminist new wave cinema, ethics in the Anthropocene and animal/human studies. Her writings have been translated into eleven languages for publication in academic journals and anthologies. She is the director of the Human Rights and Animal Ethics Research Network (HRAE). She has made several documentary films including the landmark *Homosexuality: A Film for Discussion*, 1975, recently screened for the Melbourne International Film Festival's 70th anniversary. Creed has been invited to participate in international research events, including the Courtauld Institute, the Yale Centre for British Art, and the Cultural Programs of the National Academy of the Sciences, USA. She has been on the boards of Writers Week, the Melbourne International Film Festival, Melbourne Queer Film Festivals, and served as film critic for *The Age*, *The Big Issue* and ABC Radio National.

Lisa Fuller is a Wuilli Wuilli woman born in Queensland, also descended from Wakka Wakka and Gooreng Gooreng peoples. She's lived on Ngunnawal and Ngambri lands, Canberra since 2006 where she's completing her PhD at the University of Canberra. Fuller has won several awards, including the 2017 David Unaipon Award for an Unpublished Indigenous Writer and two 2021 Aurealis Awards.

Her novel, *Ghost Bird*, received several awards including the 2020 ACT Book of the Year, the 2020 Queensland Literary Awards, and the 2020 Readings Young Adult Book Prize; and was an Honour Book in the 2020 Children's Book Council of Australia awards. Her essays, short stories and poetry appear across various publications. Fuller wears many hats including sessional academic, freelance writer and editor. Currently, she's trying to balance family, study, work and her writing dream. www.lisafuller.com.au

Elyse Goldfinch is a curator and writer living and working in Naarm/Melbourne. She has curated, co-curated and produced over twenty exhibitions across non-profit and independent spaces, collaborating with living artists to develop projects throughout the Asia-Pacific. Goldfinch is currently Curator, Public Programs and Publications, at the Australian Centre for Contemporary Art and is a co-Director at Firstdraft (2021-2023). Most recently, she was on the curatorial team which presented Marco Fusinato's *DESASTRES* for the Australian Pavilion at the 59th Venice Biennale, and Associate Editor of the accompanying publication. She previously held the position of Associate Curator at Artspace, Sydney, where she has contributed to a dynamic program of Australian and international projects and residencies.

Goldfinch has written for print and online art journals including *Ocula*, *Art & Australia*, and *un Magazine*, alongside contributing texts for monographs on Angelica Mesiti and Mel O'Callaghan, and *Know My Name*, National Gallery of Australia, 2022.

Kier-La Janisse is a film writer, producer, acquisitions executive for Severin Films and Adjunct Associate Professor in the School of Communication and Creative Arts at Deakin University. She is the author of *House of Psychotic Women: An Autobiographical Topography of Female Neurosis in Horror and Exploitation Films*, 2012/2022; and *A Violent Professional: The Films of Luciano Rossi*, 2007. Janisse has been an editor of numerous books including *Warped & Faded: Weird Wednesday and the Birth of the American Genre Film Archive*, 2021; and *Satanic Panic: Pop-Cultural Paranoia in the 1980s,* 2015. She wrote, directed and produced the award-winning documentary *Woodlands Dark and Days Bewitched: A History of Folk Horror,* 2021, and produced the acclaimed blu-ray box sets *All the Haunts Be Ours: A Compendium of Folk Horror,* 2021, and *The Sensual World of Black Emanuelle*, 2023. She is currently in development on several book and film projects. kierlajanisse.com

Alison Peirse is a Professor of Film Studies at the University of Leeds, UK. Her research specialisation focusses on horror film and feminist film historiography. She has published four books and over twenty journal articles and chapters on horror film and television. Her essays and books have won awards around the world, and her edited collection *Women Make Horror: Filmmaking, Feminism, Genre* was the subject of a screening series at the Museum of Modern Art in New York City in 2022. She is the writer, director and editor of a number of short documentaries on feminism and horror film, which have been commissioned by and/or screened at international film festivals, and have been nominated for or won numerous awards, including Winner, Best Film, Wench Film Festival, India, 2023; Winner, Best Documentary Short, GenreBlast, USA, 2023; Winner, Staff Choice Best Short Film of 2023, Visioni Notturne, Italy, 2023; Winner, Best Documentary, Galacticat Festival De Cinema Fantàstic, Spain, 2023; and Highly Commended, Delta Film Award, Festival of Fantastic Films, UK, 2023. She is currently working on her next book, *Her Chainsaw Heart: A Feminist History of Horror Film*, which is funded by a prestigious AHRC Research, Development and Engagement Fellowship.

Curators' Acknowledgements

It has been an immense honour and privilege to work with the incredible artists, contributors, colleagues and supporters who have shaped this project alongside us. We are enormously grateful for the generosity of knowledge, time, commitment and energy that has been shared. Thank you to everyone involved for making all our nightmares come true.

We extend our heartfelt thanks to each of the artists for inspiring and trusting us with their works and ideas – Naomi Blacklock, Mia Boe, Louise Bourgeois, Cybele Cox, Karla Dickens, Lonnie Hutchinson, Naomi Kantjuriny, Minyoung Kim, Maria Kozic, Jemima Lucas, Clare Milledge, Tracey Moffatt, Theron Debris, Julia Robinson, Marianna Simnett, Heather B Swann, Suzan Pitt, Kellie Wells, and Zamara Zamara. Thank you for plunging into the dark side with us.

We would like to thank publication contributors – Jessica Balazagetui, Barbara Creed, Lisa Fuller, Kier-La Janisse and Alison Peirse – for expanding the language of horror and articulating the freedom with which it can be approached. Particular thanks must be extended to Barbara Creed for enthusiastically supporting our engagement with her theory of the monstrous-feminine as a curatorial framework and for talking so openly with us about horror films and ideas. We are also delighted to have collaborated with fellow horror enthusiast Jessica Balazagetui who has been instrumental in developing the *Screams on Screen* associated programof film, talks and performance hosted at ACCA, The Capitol Theatre, and other mysterious, spooky locations across the Melbourne CBD.

From the other side would not have been possible without the unwavering support and guidance of our ACCA colleagues. The exhibition was brought to life thanks to an immensely talented and committed project team including Samantha Vawdrey, Claire Richardson, Casey Jeffrey, Shae Nagorcka, Brian Scales and Simone Tops, alongside the incredible team of installers, and technicians from Fine Art Media. A personal thanks also goes to Artistic Director & CEO, Max Delany and Senior Curator, Shelley McSpedden for providing curatorial support throughout the exhibition's development, and designer Matt Hinkley for making our gruesome vision come to life through the project's collateral and publication.

We would also like to acknowledge our gratitude for all the galleries and private collectors who have worked with us to support artists and loan work for the exhibition. Finally, our sincere thanks to Media Partners The Saturday Paper and 3RRR, Screening Program Partner City of Melbourne and RMIT Culture, and Exhibition Partner Dulux for introducing us to our favourite new colour 'tongue'.

— Elyse Goldfinch and Jessica Clark

Project Team

Curators
Elyse Goldfinch
Jessica Clark

Editor
Elyse Goldfinch

Publication Designer
Matt Hinkley

Print
Adams Print

Copyeditors
Max Delany and Jessica Clark

Exhibition Manager
Samantha Vawdrey

Project Manager
Shae Nagorcka

Installation Team
Adam John Cullen
Gala Hazell
Casey Jeffery (Team Leader)
Marty de Jesus
Brian Scales
Nicholas Smith
Simone Tops

AV specialists
Fine Art Media

Dulux Paint Colours
Tongue
Ticking
Vivid White

Staff and Donors

ACCA Board

John Denton, Chair
Dr Terry Wu, Deputy Chair
Fayen d'Evie
Sarah Lynn Rees
Andrew Taylor
Gordon Thomson

ACCA Staff

Max Delany
Artistic Director & CEO

Claire Richardson
Executive Director

Laura De Neefe
Director, Development & Engagement

Shelley McSpedden
Senior Curator

Jessica Clark
Curator

Elyse Goldfinch
Curator, Public Programs & Publications

Samantha Vawdrey
Exhibitions Manager

Margaret Stern
Operations Manager

Badra Aji
Visitor Experience Manager

Grace Fraraccio
Development & Digital Content Coordinator

Monique Chiari
Development & Marketing Assistant

Felicia Pinchen-Hogg
Education Manager

Minna Lappalainen
Education & Access Coordinator

Lauren Simmonds
Artist Educator

Maggie Lu
Accounts Coordinator

Matt Hinkley
Designer

Katrina Hall
Publicist

Visitor Experience Coordinators
Arini Byng
Monique Chiari
Ruth Cummins
Ponie Curtis
Emily Hubbard
Camille Thomas

Visitor Experience Team
Nicholas Anderson
Beatrice Gabriel
Danielle Goder
Suzannah Griffith
Dhariz Manalo
Jacinta Maude
Leah Nathan
Kirra Niner
Luka Rhoderick
Katinka Samuel
Dom Viggiani
Beatriz Airah Yu

Volunteers
Jasmine Babayan
Xiyu Bi
Meg Bielby
Alec Bolwell
Amanda Chamsay
Jess Chow
Emily Crawford

Jessica Ebeyer
Lucy Eidelson
Arty Foulkes
Flora Harpley Green
Harper Hamilton-Grutzner
Gala Hazell
Enya Hu
Jasmine Jafari
Bambi Johnson
Alissa Lad
Simone Lee
Yueyao Li
Songwen Luo
Maria McGowan
Grace Chanthicha Meekun-iam
Declan Monaghan
Julie Monaghan
Matilda Mourant
Bo-dene Mu
Amy Naylor
Lauren Nevard
Mara O'Keeffe
Elyse O'Neill
Shaarn Pateman
Phillip Patterson
China Paul
Meyrick Payne
Mikayla Poon
Yongpin Ren
Moksha Richards
Mythra Sage
Crystal Schubert
Daniel Song
CJ Starc
Sylva Storm
Andari Suherlan
Scarlet Sykes Hesterman
Josh V.E.
Chloe Vella
Indiana Wells
Sinéad Wheeler
Anna Xiang
Yuji Zou

ACCA Donors

Visionary
The Macfarlane Fund
J. Andrew Cook & Prof. Wendy Brown
Vivien & Graham Knowles

Champion
Michael & Janet Buxton
John Denton & Susan Cohn
Bruce Parncutt AO
Megan Ponsford & Noel Fermanis
Prescott Family Foundation
Michael Schwarz & David Clouston
Dr Terry Wu & Dr Melinda Tee

Guardian
Lesley Alway & Paul Hewison
Australia China Art Foundation
Sam & Tania Brougham
Rosemary Forbes & Ian Hocking
Judith & Leon Gorr
Marita & James Lillie
Emeritus Professor Margaret Plant
Frank Pollio
Craig Semple
Chris & Cheryl Thomas
Marita Onn & John Tuck
Rosemary Walls

Patron
Anthony & Michele Boscia
Paul & Samantha Cross
Georgia Dacakis
Peter & Leila Doyle
Sophie Gannon
Rachel Griffiths & Andrew Taylor
Lou & Will McIntyre
Mark Nelson
Jan van Schaik
Sarah & Ted Watts
Anonymous (2)

Friend
Lyn & Rob Backwell
Professor Andrew Benjamin
Bird de la Coeur Architects
Ingrid Braun
Jon & Gabrielle Broome
Sue Dodd
Jane Hemstritch
Alana Kushnir & Shaun Cartoon
Launch Housing
Elizabeth Leslie
Gene-Lyn Ngian & Jeffrey Robinson
Drew Pettifer
Sue Rose & Alan Segal
Susan M Renouf
Jane Ryan & Nick Kharsas
Steven Smith
Jennifer Strauss AM
Fiona Sweet & Paul Newcombe
Irene Sutton
Noel & Jenny Turnbull
Lyn Williams AM
Anonymous (5)

Contemporary
Sally Browne AM
Elly Fink
Emily Floyd
Lesa-Belle Furhagen
Vida Maria Gaigalas
Nicholas Lolatgis
Angela Rutherford & Vincenzo Giarrusso
Dr Nigel Simpson
Anonymous (5)

Enthusiast
Sandy & Damian Abrahams
Julia Gardiner
John McNamara
Kenneth W Park
Raffaele Cotroneo
Anonymous (4)

ACCA Partners and Supporters

Exhibition Partner

Dulux

Screening program partners

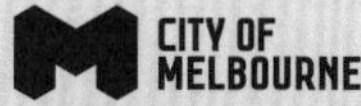

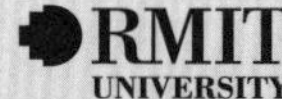

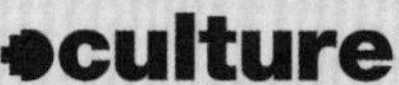

Lead Media Partner

The Saturday Paper

Media Partner

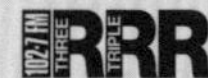

Government Partners

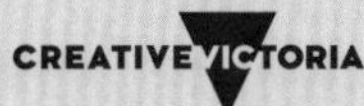

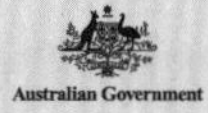

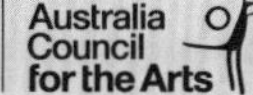

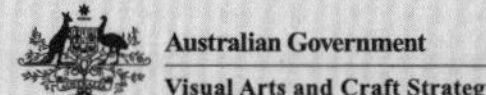

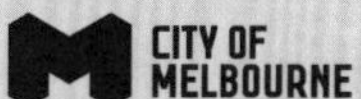

THE EDUCATION STATE

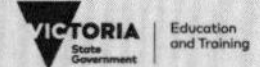

Network Partners

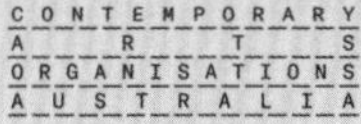

Partners

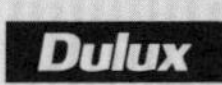

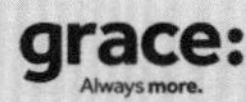

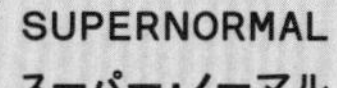

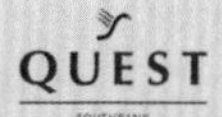

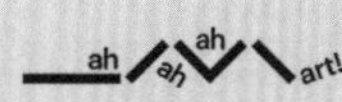

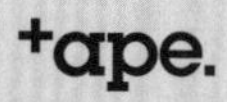

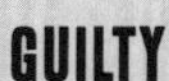

Trusts and Foundations

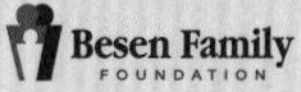

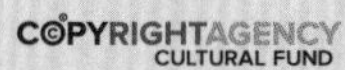

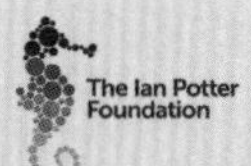

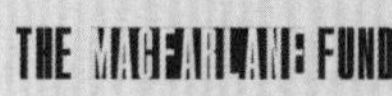

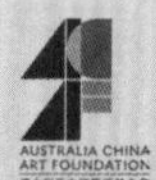

Media Partners

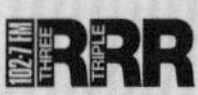

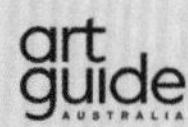

The Monthly
The Saturday Paper
7am

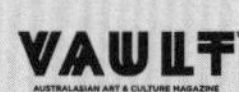

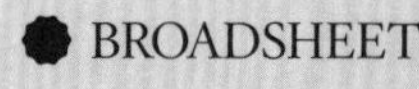

Event Partners

firecracker event.

DENTON
DENTONWINE.COM

NOISY RITUAL
URBAN WINERY

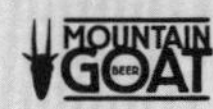

mgc
THE MELBOURNE GIN COMPANY

CAPI

Supporters

ac ANDREW CURTIS PHOTOGRAPHY

From the other side
Australian Centre for Contemporary Art
9 December 2023 – 3 March 2024

Curators: Elyse Goldfinch and Jessica Clark
Editor: Elyse Goldfinch
Published 2023

ISBN: 978-0-6458328-3-9

Australian Centre for Contemporary Art
111 Sturt Street
Southbank VIC 3006
Melbourne, Australia
acca.melbourne

Dustjacket, cover and pages:
Maria Kozic, *Calendar Girls*, 1999 (details)

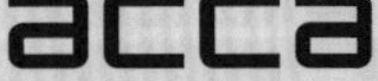

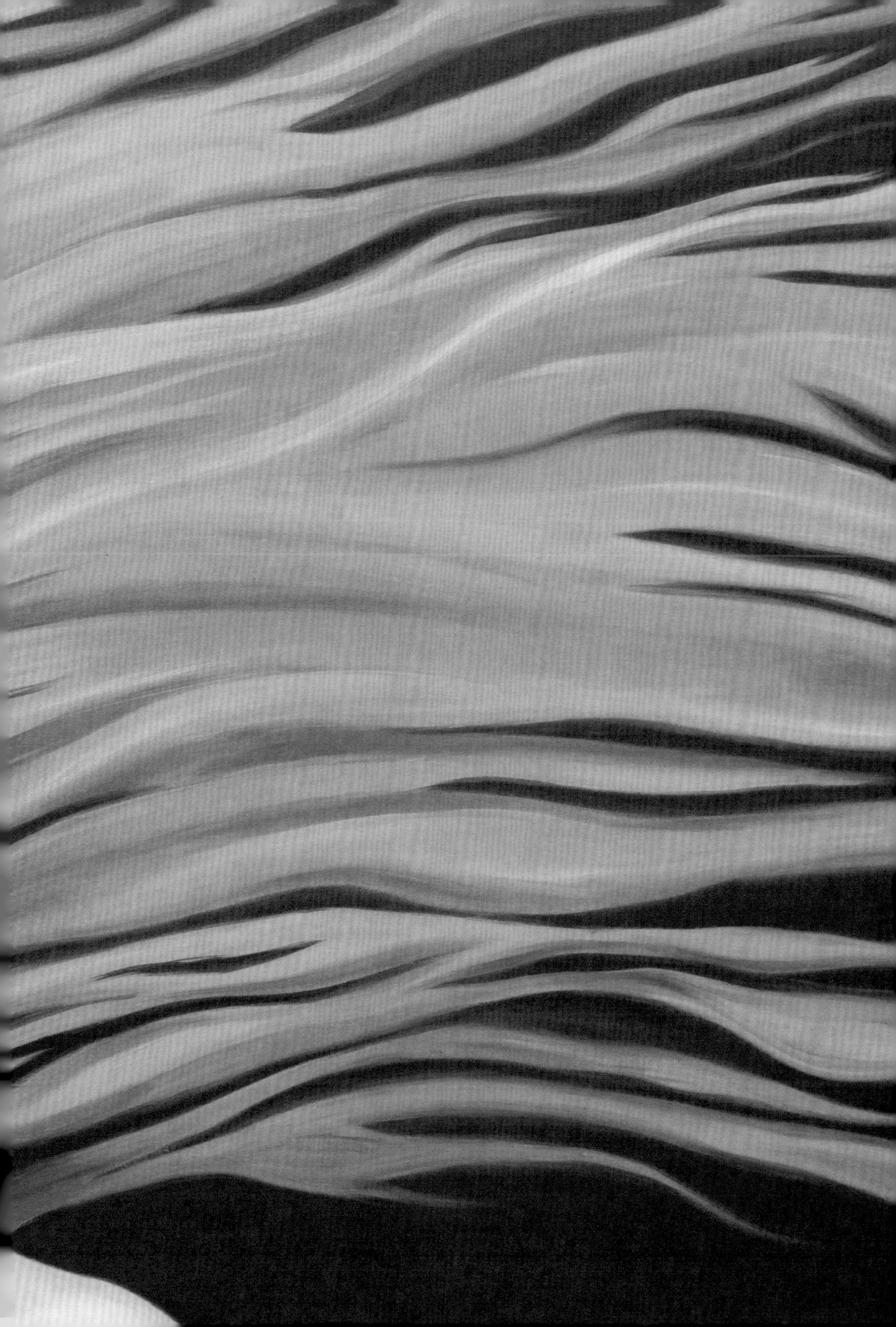

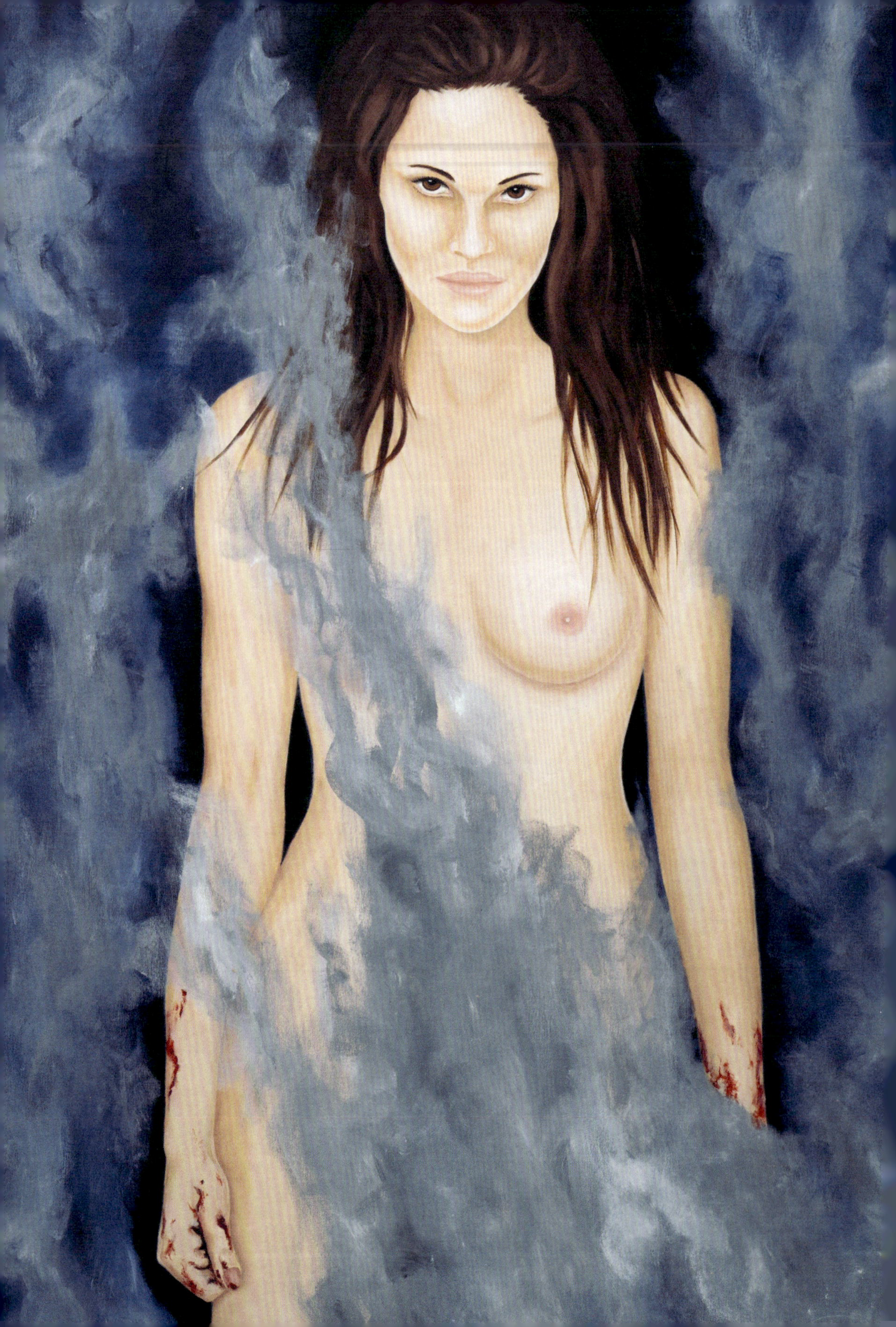

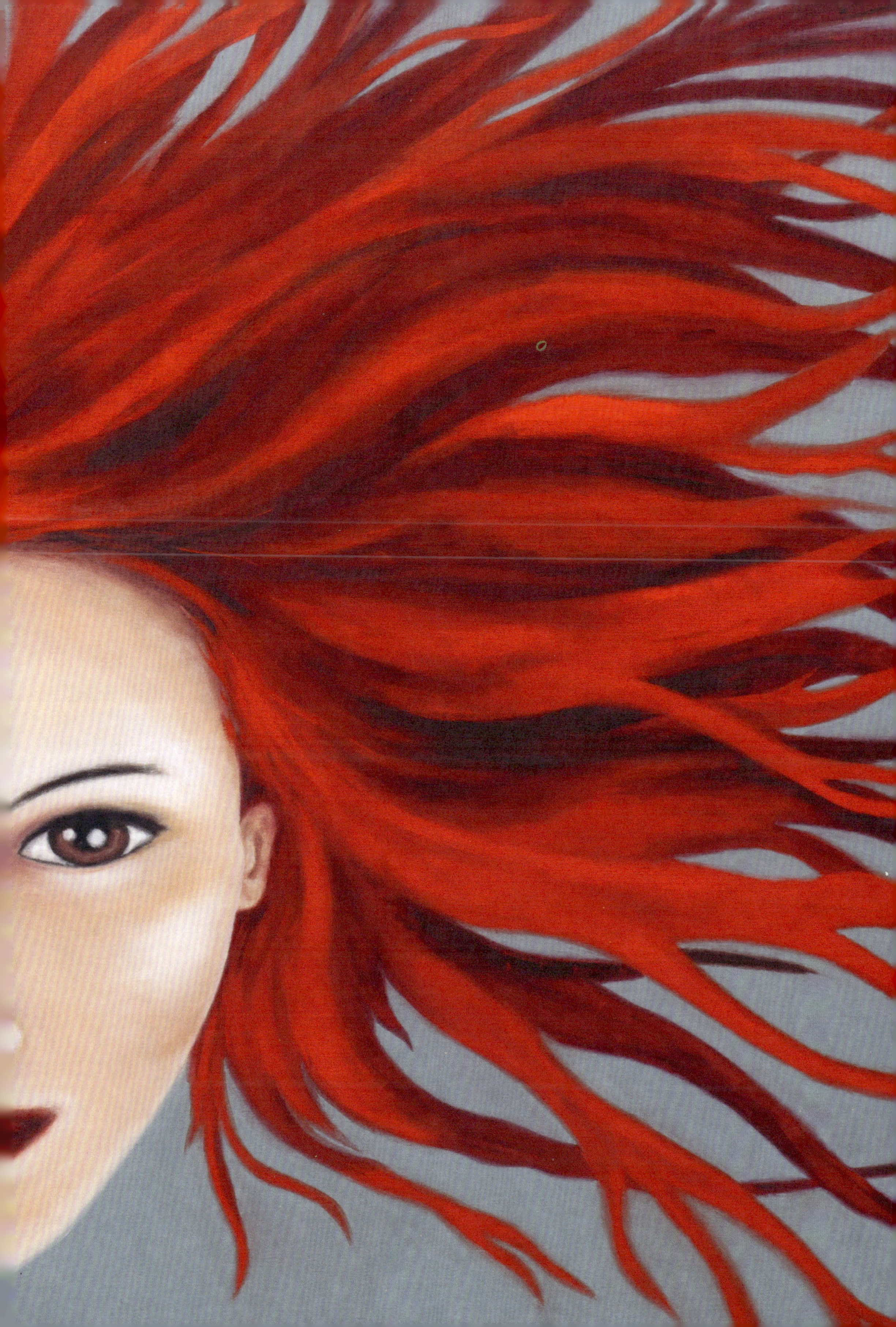

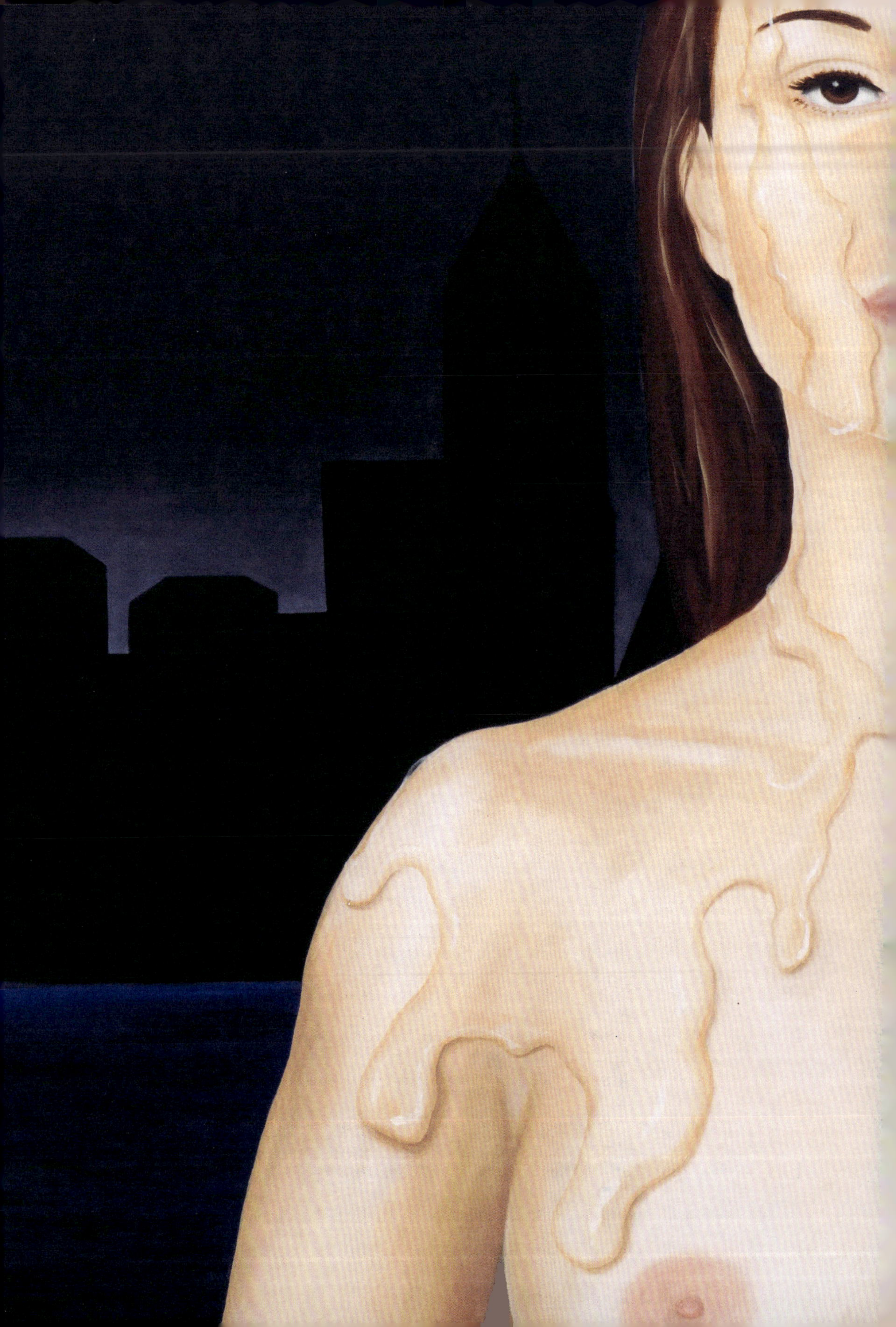